Leslie V. Knowles

Lady Dalton's Deception

A WOLVERTON WORLD NOVELLA

Copyright © 2025 by Leslie V. Knowles

All rights reserved.

No part of this publication may be reproduced, distributed, or transmitted in any form or by any means, including photocopying, recording, or other electronic or mechanical methods, without the prior written permission of the publisher, except as permitted by U.S. copyright law. For permission requests, contact leslievknowlesauthor@aol.com

NO AI TRAINING OR DATA SCRAPING: Without in any way limiting the author's [and publisher's] exclusive rights under copyright, any use oft is publication to "train" generative artificial intelligence (AI) technologies to generate text, audiobooks, and translations into any language is **expressly prohibited**. This includes scraping the internet for data from this work, any related data, or any works or data by Leslie V. Knowles. The author reserves all rights to license uses of this work for generative AI training and development of machine learning language models as well as the rights to all derivative works.

The story, all names, characters, and incidents portrayed in this production are fictitious. No identification with actual persons (living or deceased), places, buildings, and products is intended or should be inferred.

Book Cover by Leslie V. Knowles

ImageSource: Deposit Photos

1st edition 2025

Paperback ISBN 97817364935-7-1

Ebook ISBN 97817364935-6-4

About the Author

Leslie V. Knowles is an award winning author of Regency Romance books that deliver strong heroes, determined heroines, and situations that make them face their deepest fears to search for their dreams.

Often set beyond the ballrooms of London, Leslie's stories promise trust and discovery on the way to happily ever after.

If you're a fan of fish-out-of-water stories that challenge characters to fight for what they believe in and for the people they love, then you are in the right place.

For Larry.
My best friend, my lover, my husband.
I will miss you all the days of my life.

Overview

Halifax, Nova Scotia has given Lady Dalton a better life than she had in London, England.

Since fleeing her abusive husband, changing her name and claiming to be a widow, Sophie has learned that she is not as useless as Lord Dalton declared. Now known as Mrs. Bennett, her deception has allowed her to survive by establishing a school for young ladies which means she must protect her reputation at all costs. Over the past two years she has begun to feel safe from discovery, but she still fears what will happen if her secret is exposed.

Alec Graham is intrigued by his reserved neighbor. Gossip says she is the granddaughter of an earl and the widow of an officer who died fighting Napoleon. But why did she come to Halifax where she has no family or friends other than the housekeeper who came with her?

Shadows cloud her eyes though she is young, beautiful, and gracious. Still, she resists his attempts to charm. Perhaps now that his niece is one of her students he will learn why she is so wary of his interest.

What will it take to banish the shadows and lighten her smile?

Contents

1. Chapter 1 — 1
2. Chapter 2 — 12
3. Chapter 3 — 22
4. Chapter 4 — 30
5. Chapter 5 — 38
6. Chapter 6 — 46
7. Chapter 7 — 55
8. Chapter 8 — 64
9. Chapter 9 — 74
10. Chapter 10 — 81
11. Chapter 11 — 92
12. Chapter 12 — 101
13. Chapter 13 — 109
14. Chapter 14 — 117
15. Chapter 15 — 125
16. Chapter 16 — 130

17. Chapter 17	137
18. Chapter 18	142
Also by	144
Biography	145

Chapter 1

Halifax, Nova Scotia, Fall, 1812

Heavy rain drummed against the office windowpane of Mrs. Bennett's Academy for Young Ladies where the solitary lamp on the desk barely lifted the morning's gloom. Sophie, owner and headmistress, closed her ledger, cleaned her pen, and leaned back in her chair with a relieved sigh. She had not dared face another winter without repairing the roof though the expense worried her greatly.

The wind howled as it swept past the window and rattled the panes, but to her relief, they remained airtight and would not need to be re-glazed this year. The office reflected genteel refinement but far less grandeur than the Mayfair townhouse she had escaped two years ago. Her eyes swept over the student samplers of embroidery and framed watercolors that decorated the blue papered walls. Who would ever have believed someone as weak-willed and incompetent as her husband had declared her to be would dare to instruct young women in proper etiquette and home management?

Her former maid turned housekeeper, Margery, sat in one of the two chintz covered wingback chairs that faced her desk, her lower lip caught between her teeth. "How bad is it?"

"The repairs reduced our reserves more than I'd like but, for the moment, the school is solvent." Sophie glanced toward the heavy deluge beyond the glass. "Of course, now that the weather has turned, attendance will drop while expenses rise."

She rubbed her ink-stained fingers with a handkerchief. If only she could remove her never-ending doubts as easily as she did the ink. But the leaking roof had made her admit that her need for emergency funds outweighed her reluctance to face additional financial risks. "So, while it will further strain the budget in the short term, I agree it is time to furnish the upper rooms for boarding students. The room and board will reduce losses from inclement weather."

Her assessment of the school's monetary constraints caused Margery to lower her gaze and smooth her woolen skirts in a gesture Sophie recognized. She'd not failed to notice other signs that revealed Margery's disquiet emotions of late, so she broached the question she feared to ask, but knew she must. "Will you return to England with Mr. Farnsworth when he goes home this spring?"

Margery gasped and looked up.

In the months since Mr. Farnsworth arrived in Halifax to broker timber for his family's mining interests his attention to Margery had alarmed Sophie more than she liked. "I've seen the way you look at each other." Sophie kept her voice light lest Margery think she disapproved. She didn't. But the possibility of Margery leaving Halifax made her throat ache.

When Sophie noticed Mr. Farnsworth's interest in her friend, she had watched him for subtle warning signs she had not recognized during her own courtship. Those quickly forgiven slights and embarrassments that she had ignored in the glow of infatuation for her handsome fiancé.

LADY DALTON'S DECEPTION

But Margery had better instincts than Sophie. She did not mistake flattery for esteem or handsome looks as a promise of goodness. Sophie only wished Mr. Farnsworth were a local man who would not take her friend away.

She made herself smile. "I hope you have more sense than to deny your own happiness out of concern for me. I think Mr. Farnsworth cares a great deal for you."

Margery blinked and her eyes glistened with unshed tears. "Mr. Farnsworth is a good man, but it don't feel right to leave you all alone."

Sophie didn't know how she would have managed if her former maid had not chosen to accompany her to Halifax. Nova Scotia was very different from England. "Nevertheless, you must accept his offer if he makes one." She stopped when Margery's hands gripped the cloth she had so recently smoothed. "He already has, hasn't he?"

Margery nodded.

"Tell me you said yes."

"I wanted to, but I just couldn't." The tears spilled down Margery's cheeks. "With the roof expenses, and after Miss Thompson left to get married so sudden-like, it didn't feel right to add to your troubles." She met Sophie's gaze and bit her lip again. "But I couldn't say no, either." She looked down, then admitted, "I told him I'd think about it."

Her devotion made Sophie ashamed of her selfish fears. "Tell him yes, and don't worry about me. I can never repay you for your support when we fled my home, but you deserve to find your own way now." She came around the desk and eased Margery's hands from the twisted cloth of her skirts, then hugged her. "I wish you all the happiness you deserve and more."

Margery hugged her back. "You deserve to be happy, too," she declared. "One day you'll—"

"You know that isn't possible," Sophie interrupted her.

"Widows are free to marry," Margery argued. "You have a new name and a new life in a new world. No one here knows... and you could be happy."

"But I would know."

It hurt to know. The single dance she'd accepted with their neighbor, Mr. Graham, when she and Margery attended an assembly proved that. His obvious attraction and light conversation resurrected physical desire, but triggered alarm bells. His tall solid build, squared jaw, broad smile and warm caramel colored eyes made her heart skitter and goose flesh race down her spine. Was she still a fool for handsome men and surface impressions? She berated herself for being drawn to the easy smile that invited her to smile back.

Mr. Graham seemed courteous, kind and engaging but she no longer trusted her instincts. Even if she were willing to ignore her conscience, she dared not ignore how her husband had convinced her of his charm, only to reveal his true nature once they were married.

Sophie returned to her chair and rearranged the papers on her desk into another neat pile. "I could not take the chance of treading that path again."

Of course, none of those things mattered since she was not really a widow at all.

The sharp tang of printer's ink, mixed with the slight mustiness of newsprint, assailed Alec Graham's nose when he entered the newspaper office of the Halifax Chronical. He approached the clerk and pitched his voice to rise above the clatter of the presses at the back of the building. "Henry, I need you to place this in the next edition."

"Certainly, sir." The clerk set aside the well-worn book of poetry he held, took the paper and scanned it, his lips moving ever so slightly as he read the words. He nodded his bald head and looked up. "Right, then. It'll save me from finding a second poem for the Poet's corner."

"I doubt readers will object to or even notice the reduction."

Henry chuckled. "Someone always objects to something, Mr. Graham. It's the nature of folks."

"Sad, but true."

Alec turned to leave but stopped when Mrs. Bennett, came through the door. His home occupied the lot behind hers, so they sometimes exchanged pleasantries, but while she was gracious enough, she had never encouraged friendlier interaction. Gossip said she was the granddaughter of an earl and the widow of an officer who'd been an early casualty on the Peninsula.

The cold had pinkened her nose and cheeks, and flecks of snow dusted the hood and shoulders of her brown woolen cloak. The effect made him curl his hands lest he give in to the urge to tuck her close and carry her off to parts unknown and undisturbed.

The petite blond had attracted him with her delicate features and slender figure from their first introduction. But though she danced with him once, he quickly deduced that Mrs. Bennett was as uninterested in him as a man as he was all too aware of her as a woman.

She claimed she did not look for another husband, and her determined and unbending propriety signaled she did not want a lover either. Her blue eyes, deep and dark as a mountain pool, always seemed to observe the world with wary caution.

He inclined his head in polite recognition. "Good morning, Mrs. Bennett."

She returned his greeting with an answering nod before passing him to speak to Henry. "I should like to place this notice in the next edition if I may."

"Of course, Mrs. Bennett." Henry replied. "If I postpone the Poet's Corner until next week I believe it can still be included in tomorrow's edition."

She pursed her lips and a crease formed between her eyebrows. "My students are encouraged to discuss the poems in each edition, and poetry is a welcome relief from the serious concerns of war and shipping news. If it will mean the loss of the Poet's Corner tomorrow, I believe my notice can wait for next week's edition."

"Or perhaps a shorter poem can be found to fit," Alec suggested.

Her eyes widened, the crease disappeared, and for a brief moment, he thought she might smile, but she merely said, "An excellent suggestion, Mr. Graham." Then she turned her attention back to Henry. "Would that be possible? Also, perhaps I can word the notice more succinctly." Once they agreed on new wording, she paid Henry, said farewell to Alec, and took her leave without further comment.

Alec experienced the usual pang of disappointment that she did not linger in conversation. The lady intrigued him.

Careful and refined as her behavior was in company, Alec had glimpsed moments when she thought herself unobserved. That was how he knew she fed scraps of food to the stray cats and dogs who occasionally took shelter under her back porch. He sometimes heard her and her housekeeper laughing together, though never when others were present. He had watched her in the yard from his upstairs window one day when she twirled in circles with her face to the sun and eyes closed while she sang off key.

Behind him, Henry uttered a murmured, "Aha."

Alec smiled, then exited and returned to the waterfront.

Water Street bustled with activity from Captain Peabody's newly arrived merchant ship and Alec greeted several acquaintances along the way. Wagons loaded with goods rattled past and friendly banter filled the air along with dog barks and the clang of ship's bells. Seagulls swooped and screeched in protest when workers disturbed their attempts to raid fish carts on the dock. The salt-tang of brine blended with the exotic scent of imported spices from the West Indies.

In the half dozen years since he'd come to Halifax from his brother's farm to broker the family's timber interests, he'd discovered he had a talent for negotiating trade and had invested in several shipping ventures. His brother Rory teased him that it wasn't so much a talent for negotiation that contributed to his successes but his intimidating scowl when things didn't go his way. He didn't know about the scowl, but he did know that he preferred running the town-based business to the isolation of the logging and farm life he'd left behind.

Alec strode past the wide ground level doors of the warehouse where timber was stored and climbed the stairs to the upper floor and his office. This level shared its space with goods from distant ports and the aroma of spice mingled with those of fabrics and foreign artifacts. He hung his hat and overcoat on a wall peg, then crossed to his desk.

A great orange cat lay draped across the scattered stacks of papers he'd left behind. Alec lifted the beast from the pile. "Sorry, Clyde, but I have work to do." He scratched the cat behind the ears before setting him down. "Go earn your keep and catch some rats." At Alec's feet, Clyde stretched before raising his tail in the air and sauntering off to curl up in a shaft of light from the window.

Alec reached for the pile of correspondence he'd sorted before leaving the office. Most were reports from acquaintances who kept him informed of the latest news about the hostilities between England and France or the American states. According to those reports, it was General Wellington's pursuit of the French in Spain that held the king's attention and not Mr. Madison's most recent protests and his declaration of war against England. He doubted the complaints of the former colonies made much impact on the crown when compared to Napoleon and his quest to dominate the continent. Fortunately, Alec's business interests benefited from the influx of His Majesty's navy ships in the harbor.

He reached for the stack, then frowned when he saw the black-edged letter that had not been on the pile when he left. A cold shiver of dread ran down his spine. Accidents happened too often to ignore but, please, God, *no more family.* His brother, Rory's, wife died in a freak accident five years ago.

The letter was short but he only focused on two words. *Papa. Drowned.* His mind shut down, numbed by shock while ice shards of grief splintered his heart. He sagged back against the chair, his fingers letting the paper slide to the floor. *Not Rory.*

Images filled his head. Rory laughing uproariously after playing a practical joke on him. Rory laying a consoling arm around Alec's shoulder after he'd failed to win a local horse race. Rory beaming with pride when he'd stood in front of Alec's warehouse after delivering the first timbers to be brokered by his little brother. Always cheerful, positive and supportive.

His big brother was larger than life. Rory was careful. Rory was skilled. Rory was... *dead.*

Another memory rose up and his breath hitched. Rory, white-faced and red-eyed after Janet's mother died. But Rory's eight-year-old daughter had needed him so he had hugged her and told her she now had two parents in one. Any other grieving had been done in private. Now it was Rory who was dead and Alec's own eyes burned, his throat ached, and his stomach threatened to rebel.

Alec picked the letter off the floor and studied it, disturbed to see young Janet had written it. Alarm bells rang in his head to see the date. *Two weeks ago*? With Rory gone she would be all alone. *She's just a child.*

He grabbed his coat and hat from the peg, rushed down the stairs, and called to the man directing the unloading of the wagons and carts below. "Mr. Pike, you are in charge until I return."

He opened the door to his house and stopped dead at the sight of the bedraggled youth who sat beside the fireplace that heated his residence. A burlap bag rested beside the chair.

"Hello, Uncle Alec."

Janet? It took him a moment to reconcile this girl-woman dressed in boy's clothing with the elfin faced child he pictured when he thought of his niece. *No longer a child.*

She sat stiffly, Clyde's calico sibling asleep on her lap. Her eyes reflected a world of grief. How long since he'd seen her? Four years ago Rory brought Janet to Halifax for her ninth birthday but Alec had not been to the farm since that Christmas. He had meant to go last year... and the year before that. His stomach cramped and his chest locked. He would never be able to visit Rory again.

Rory is dead and Janet is my responsibility.

He opened his arms.

Janet leapt into them and pressed her face against his shoulder with a muffled sob. "I didn't know what else to do."

They stood together for several minutes. What did he know about taking care of a child, even a half-grown one? How old was she now? Thirteen? No, fourteen, last August.

"Who brought you?"

"I brought myself."

Dear God. She had traveled alone?

Male clothing had allowed her to pass as a young lad and made her less noticeable, but it was no protection against the hazards of backcountry beasts or the storms of the past week. What if something had happened to her? He would not have known to look for her. He tightened his hold and lowered his chin to the top of her head. "You should have waited for me. I would have come sooner, but the letter just arrived. "

"I know. I put it there."

She pulled back. Her tears were gone, though her eyes were pink-rimmed. "The house was too empty... like it had died with Papa. I had to get away. I found the key you gave

Papa and left." Her gaze held both uncertainty and bravado. Her voice quivered and a tear rolled down her face. "Did I do the right thing?"

Chapter 2

The aroma of spiced cakes greeted Sophie when she arrived back at the academy after completing her business with the newspaper followed by a visit to the pawn broker. The earbobs were the last of the jewels she'd brought with her to her new life and she was pleased that they had garnered enough to pay for the necessary furnishings for student bedchambers.

Margery always prepared fresh treats to be included with their afternoon lessons so the girls learned the practical nuances of eating in public. At least that was how Sophie explained the sweets that rewarded a week of lessons well learned. In reality, she had a sweet tooth and it was one of the few indulgences she allowed herself.

"Were you able to reach satisfactory terms with the broker?" Margery asked when Sophie stepped into the kitchen.

"Yes. I have a year in which to redeem the earbobs. If I take in at least four boarding students, I should be able to reclaim them by then. If I fill six rooms I shall reclaim them within eight months." She hung her cloak on a peg near the door. "I placed notices in the newspaper for staff and to announce that I would be taking in boarding students."

She didn't mention her encounter with Mr. Graham. He had been leaving the news office when she entered. A warm flush flowed up from her middle and heated her cheeks. His suggestion meant he had eavesdropped though he had no reason to thrust himself into their conversation. It troubled her to realize she had been pleased that he had. Worry tightened her throat. *Too pleased.*

She reached for a slice of cake, broke it into two pieces, offered half to Margery and shifted her thoughts away from her silliness. "I hope whoever replaces you in the kitchen bakes as well as you. Try as I may, I still produce as many failures as successes."

"You were not raised to work in kitchens." Margery chuckled as she took the piece of cake. "Though you've learned a lot since leaving England."

When the clock struck the half-hour, Sophie finished her cake and dusted her fingers. "I'd best prepare for class. Fortunately, the snow is light and most of the girls should attend this afternoon's session. Amelia Dowling's family is hosting a dinner party for several newly arrived dignitaries at the end of the week, so I'll need to review precedence and protocol today."

As soon as she arrived for class Miss Dowling announced that she'd caught a glimpse of one of the unmarried officers who was part of the delegation who *was oh so handsome.* She was to have a new dress for the occasion and was to act as hostess with the tea. Duly impressed with the prospect of displaying their accomplishments to the visiting dignitaries, they all paid close attention to Sophie's lessons.

All in all, their happy excitement cheered Sophie as well. She had been every bit as giddy as Amelia Dowling when her guardian's wife had taken her shopping for her first ball gown. She sometimes forgot how lighthearted she'd once been.

The afternoon sunlight had faded when Sophie dismissed her class and waved them on their way. She returned to the kitchen where Margery sat by the worktable knitting a scarf of bright red. It would be a gift to give one of the students for Christmas. Sophie had a half finished one of dark green in her workbasket tucked in the corner of the drawing room.

Margery looked up and asked, "Do you suppose that *oh so handsome* unmarried officer knows the Dowlings have a marriageable daughter?"

"If he doesn't he is too dim-witted to be on a diplomatic mission." Sophie chuckled.

A knock at the door caught them by surprise and Margery rose and left the kitchen. She returned a moment later, her expression one of barely suppressed curiosity. "Mr. Graham is here to see you. He is in your office."

This morning's encounter rose up to disturb her emotions again. His chiseled features and tall, powerful presence fascinated her at the same time as they repelled her. She was no longer that foolish girl who had not understood that physical appeal held no more promise of kindness than the tale that rainbows led to pots of gold. Attraction was not honor. Impressive physique could prove cruel.

Even if she were free to explore a relationship, she knew better than to fall prey to carnal desire a second time. It was too fleeting. It was too dangerous. Sophie straightened her spine and forced herself to resist her unwelcome reaction. She entered the office and took a calming breath before she stepped behind her desk.

"Miss Chandler said you wish to speak with me, Mr. Graham?"

He stood facing the window, his hands clasped behind his back, his stance one of restrained energy. He turned, and

Sophie flinched. His scowl lowered his brow and his intense gaze froze her heartbeat.

What did I — ?

She blinked and refocused.

No. Not me-- but something.

Her automatic assumption that she was to blame for whatever upset him shocked her. She'd thought she had put those old habits behind her when she came to Halifax. She pushed down the deep-rooted fears, bit the inside of her cheek and raised her chin. She would not be cowed by a man she barely knew.

"I'm sorry to intrude, Mrs. Bennett, but I am in need of a favor."

Despite his fierce expression, his words were calm and entirely unexpected. It took her a moment to digest their meaning. A favor? He needs a favor *from me?* The concept threw her off balance. She had always been the one in need of assistance.

She sank into her chair and gestured for him to take the seat opposite the desk, then folded her hands and rested them on the desk to prevent him from noticing their tremor. Sophie swallowed to moisten her throat. She was relieved when her voice sounded calm and curious instead of shaken and timid. "What can I do for you, sir?"

Mr. Graham seated himself but still looked ready to spring up and pace the room. His hands gripped the armrests on his chair as though holding himself in place. "This afternoon I learned that my brother recently died." He held up a hand and continued before she could express condolences. "Both the news of his death and my niece arrived together and I am in a quandary. I am now her guardian and have no idea what to do with or for a girl nearing marriageable age."

He answered her question before she could ask.

"She is fourteen."

His lips turned down and his forehead creased. "My upper rooms are currently rented by a ship's captain who arrived in Halifax last week so I cannot house her with me until he leaves port. I would give her my room and make a pallet for myself in the kitchen, but the captain's presence creates a problem. He is unmarried and will be in Halifax for the next month."

Aha. "And thus the favor you need is for me to house your niece?"

Sophie watched the dull red creep up and spread across the broad cheekbones and all the way to his hairline. His embarrassment struck her as a surprising vulnerability. He must hate asking for help. His hands left the armrests and he smoothed them along his knees, then clamped them back on the chair.

"I should also like to enroll her in your school. My brother taught her to read and do sums but she doesn't know the things you teach." His lips firmed and he drilled her with a determined gaze. "She may seem a bit rough since she has had very little exposure to feminine influence, but Janet is a clever girl."

Sophie looked down at her clasped hands. She flexed her fingers, then lowered her hands to her lap. "I realize you know I plan to take boarding students, but I am not yet ready for them, Mr. Graham. I have no beds other than my housekeeper's and my own.

He stood and paced over to the window that faced the back of his residence. "I can provide her with a cot from my warehouse." His voice roughened and he cleared his throat. "Janet has had a difficult time of it, Mrs. Bennett. She lost her mother when she was eight. The farm is isolated and she had to make do more often than not. She is a practical girl who has slept in rough conditions when necessary. She will not balk at using a cot for a few days." He turned away from the window. "I know it is a lot to ask on such short notice, but I ask anyway. Will you allow me to bring her to you tonight?"

When she'd put her plan into motion this morning Sophie had allowed herself a month to furnish and plan for the change. She wasn't ready. She had ordered furnishings this morning, but she had yet to prepare schedules and rules. She'd followed strict rules at the school her trustees sent her to after her parents died.

Sophie bit her lip. *Fourteen years old.*

Nearly the same age she'd been when her parents had died. She had been frightened and so very alone. "Very well, Mr. Graham. She may sleep on the cot until there is a proper bed."

The tense set of his jaw eased and his shoulders relaxed. "Thank you. If I may, I shall bring her to you after supper." He smiled broadly. "I hope I can call on you for guidance in procuring clothing and books she will require. She brought very little with her."

Sophie swallowed hard. The hulking man whose scowl intimidated her when she entered her office now possessed far more charm than was safe under any circumstances. She willed her pulse to slow and her cheeks to cool. Mr. Graham's actions were as changeable as her husband's had been. Had Dalton's mercurial moods taught her nothing? Manners, however, demanded she respond positively.

"I will do what I can, Mr. Graham." Sophie stood and came around the desk to signal the end of their discussion. She needed the next hour to think. She needed the next hour to prepare. She needed the next hour to armor herself against the onslaught of feelings she'd thought long buried.

Oh, Lord, what have I done?

Alec returned to his house to find the young girl-woman sitting beside the hearth no longer resembled a vagrant boy. With her face scrubbed free of travel dirt and her thick black hair brushed into braids, she looked like the sturdy farm girl she was. Her simple indigo blue woolen dress might have fit her properly when it was made, but she had clearly matured and grown since then. She was on the cusp of womanhood and he hadn't a clue what to do with or for her.

"Are you hungry? I'll put the kettle on for tea water."

"'Tis already on the hob. I found some bread and an apple to eat with the pemmican I still had with me. It was enough."

His larder held the basics of bread, cheese, fruit, and tea, but little else. "I'm sorry there weren't more staple goods for you. I usually take my meals at the local inn, so I don't keep much here." Alec went to the wall cupboard and located the crock containing the India tea he preferred. He took down a plain brown teapot from the shelf and measured a portion of tea leaves, then used a towel to lift the steaming kettle from the hearth and pour the water over them. Once he filled the mugs and handed one to Janet, he moved the second ladder-back chair so he could face her.

"Now that you are refreshed from your travels, we need to discuss practical matters."

Her lip quivered and she eyed him like a rabbit watched a fox on the prowl, and damned if he didn't feel as though he was about to kill her hopes. *How can I explain?*

"Much as I might wish otherwise, you will not be able to stay with me right now." He held up his hand when tears welled in her eyes. He hated the look of dismay his words produced. He must seem to be rejecting her when she most needed support.

"My upper floor is let to Captain Peabody until the end of the month, so I have arranged for you to stay at the Academy for Young Ladies on the street behind this one. The head mistress, Mrs. Bennett, is expanding her school to take boarding students and has agreed to enroll you. That way I will be nearby and you will have a safe place to stay."

He cleared his throat. "She decided to make the changes quite recently so there won't be a true bed for you to sleep on tonight but you will have a proper bed soon."

Janet bit her lip, blinked, and then pulled herself into the stiff posture Alec recognized as wounded pride. "If you do not want me here I shall return home. Ian McInnis offered to marry me and to take over the farm so--"

"That is not what I said." Alec leapt up, pulled her from the chair and wrapped his arms around her in a tight hug. "I am sorry you must reside with Mrs. Bennett for now, but I want you here." He eased back and scowled. "And you are far too young to marry, lass."

"I'd not be the first to marry young. I heard girls can marry at twelve."

"Only when a parent or guardian agrees, and I'll not agree. It will be at least four years before I will consider such a thing for you." He raised her chin to make her look at him. "If this McInnis fellow shows up looking for you I will make sure he knows that." He scowled. "How old is he?"

"I don't rightly know. He was a friend of Papa's."

"Then, not only are you too young to marry but he is too old for you."

She met his gaze without flinching. "He helped Papa with the farm, and promised to help me, too. He said we'd have to marry if he took over since he couldn't stay at the house with Papa gone. I told him if needs must, I'd do it. But I wasn't quite ready." After a moment, her lips curved into a smile and she wiped her eyes. "Then I decided to come find you, so I'm glad I don't have to."

She broke away and headed toward the bedroom. "If I must attend this academy to remain in Halifax, then I shall." She returned with the bedraggled clothing she'd arrived in and rolled them into a ball before stuffing them into the bag that had held her dress. "Is Mrs. Bennett awfully old? The only old lady I ever met was mean and cranky."

Alec chuckled. "No, she is not old."

"What is she like?"

Alec hesitated. What was Mrs. Bennett like? Pleasant. Attractive. *Very attractive*, though he'd not say so to Janet. He really knew very little other than what she had told her students' families. He had glimpsed a lighter, more playful side than she showed the world, but why she hid it he did not know.

"She is a young widow. She came to Halifax after her husband was killed fighting the French two or three years ago. She is well accepted by respectable families and, from what I've heard, her students like and respect her as well."

LADY DALTON'S DECEPTION

"But what is she *like*?" Janet pulled the drawstrings tight on her bag and turned to him. "What makes her laugh? Does she like music or dancing? Will she talk to me or just give me orders? Is she nice or is she simply a necessary place for me to stay?"

Alec drained his mug. The things that intrigued him about Mrs. Bennett were not things he could share with his niece. Janet's questions echoed other things he'd like to know. With Janet enrolled in the school he'd have a chance to find out.

"I don't know much more than what I told you. Other than charitable works, she doesn't socialize a great deal. She is careful of her reputation and that of her school, but she is pleasant to talk to. You will have to decide for yourself what she is like."

And when you do, tell me

Chapter 3

Days later, Sophie closed the door to her office and leaned against it. Her stomach churned and tension cramped her neck muscles until her skull ached from the effort to appear calm in the midst of chaos. Her students had arrived, flighty with anticipation for the dinner party scheduled tomorrow evening. Since all the girls had been invited, their spirited excitement made it difficult to keep them focused. She'd dealt with two hours of stifled giggles and distracted fidgeting before deliverymen brought the furnishings she'd ordered and she bowed to the inevitable to send the girls home. There was no point trying to counter the prospect of attracting the interest of *oh so handsome* officers who would also attend the dinner party. *Officers recently arrived from England.*

Unease made her breath hitch as it did every time a ship arrived, even though it was unlikely to bring anyone who knew Dalton. Nor was she likely to be introduced to any of the new arrivals. She was a schoolmistress, not a lady of social standing.

She massaged the back of her neck. The girls had just left when Margery slipped on the stairs and twisted her ankle while directing the deliverymen. The injury was not serious, but Sophie sent her to her room to rest it for the remainder of the day. With Margery laid up, Sophie had sorted the linens, divided them among the new bedchambers, set candles into the holders, and settled the water pitchers and bowls on their washstands.

Then, as if that were not enough, Mr. Graham had arrived with another collection of imported cloth to be turned into dresses for his niece. Miss Graham had brought only two dresses, and neither of them fit her properly. Sophie knew how spiteful some people could be to anyone whose appearance did not fit their standards, so she had taken the girl to the seamstress for fittings and delayed her introduction to her classmates until the dresses were ready.

When she explained this to Mr. Graham, he had agreed to his niece receiving private lessons until the seamstress could complete at least two dresses. Unfortunately, the man had become a disturbing part of her life by delivering the very finest of the cloth goods from his warehouse on a daily basis.

The way her body warmed and pulse quickened whenever Mr. Graham arrived dismayed and embarrassed her. It disconcerted her to realize she desired the physical intimacy she had experienced before her husband turned pleasure into fear. Mr. Graham's frequent visits left her deeply unsettled every time. It mortified her that she yearned for such intimacies, and more so that she sometimes had dreams of them *with him.*

She sighed. And what to do with his niece?

Noises overhead told her that Miss Graham had chosen to shift the furniture in her room to her own satisfaction. The girl was unpolished and far more independent than any girl Sophie had ever dealt with. She was also clever, practical, and blunt. Sophie doubted Miss Graham would ever become the woman of docile refinement expected of the rest of her charges. Her childhood had been too rooted in the harsh truths of farm life.

Sophie crossed to her desk and picked up the newspaper Mr. Graham had included with his delivery. She smiled when she noted that the Poet's Corner was prominently displayed and that the poem was Alexander Pope's *A Certain Woman at Court*. She recognized the theme of admiration for a female friend and flushed. Was the poem choice mere chance by the clerk or had Mr. Graham suggested it after she accepted his niece as a boarding student? Either way, the simple gesture eased the tension at her temples.

At least the workmen had completed their tasks and Miss Graham was occupied for the time being. The near quiet after giddy girls and thumping furniture tempted her to ignore the chores still to be done.

Just five minutes.

She rested her chin on her hands and closed her eyes. She couldn't take more than that before she checked on Margery... and Miss Graham.

A light knock on the door startled her and Sophie jerked awake.

"Mrs. Bennett?"

She glanced at the clock. *Ten minutes, not five.* "Come in."

Miss Graham opened the door and crossed to the desk to hand her a folded letter. "This message arrived from the Poor Asylum for you. The woman who brought it looks tired and sickly, so I put her in the kitchen while she waits for your answer."

Sophie broke the seal and scanned the note from the Asylum's director. The man assured her that the candidate he'd sent to apply for work was undernourished but not diseased and was willing to take on any task Sophie required.

"You may send her to me, Miss Graham." She smiled as she folded the message and put it in the drawer. "And thank you for answering the door."

Moments later, Sophie understood the director's note and Miss Graham's reaction. The small woman who entered her office was bird-bone thin with great brown eyes, dull curly hair twisted into a tight knot at her neck, and a dress far too large for her tiny frame. The dress was clean but had seen many washings before being passed along to her. Her emaciated form and dull hair made her look much older than Sophie suspected her to be. Was it truly just poor nutrition that dulled the deep brown of her complexion and sharpened the hollow of her cheekbones?

The woman bobbed a curtsey and moved to stand at the front of Sophie's desk. "Good afternoon, My Lady. My name is Nettie Turner and I can clean and sew." She spoke as though she had memorized her speech and practiced it several times on the way from the asylum.

Nettie's respectful salutation caught Sophie off guard. She had abandoned her title when she assumed her false name and new life. "I am not your lady. I am Mrs. Bennett or Ma'am."

Nettie's eyes widened at her curt correction, and Sophie moderated her tone.

"How long have you been at the asylum and how did you come to be there, Nettie?"

Nettie pulled her posture tighter and her gaze shifted. "I got to Halifax a week ago. My uncle sent me to live with a cousin, but she weren't where he said she was and there was nowhere else to go."

"Where are you from?"

"I can't rightly say." Her voice held a tremor but she looked back at Sophie and declared, "I've lived all around but never in one place long enough to say I'm from there." Her voice firmed. "But I've worked hard no matter where I've been."

"Have you ever worked as a maid before?"

"No, Ma'am, but I've known girls who were maids and I can do everything they did."

A note of defiance lay beneath Nettie's voice despite her deferential manner. Sophie admired that spark of determination and the courage it took to defend herself and her situation. But how long would it be before Nettie was strong enough to fulfill the duties the position required? She couldn't afford to take on anyone who could not do the work. Nettie looked far too weak for the heavy cleaning duties boarders would create. Sophie should send her back to the asylum and hope someone more suited answered the advertisement she'd placed in the newspaper.

She should.

Nettie was too unsuitable. She was too small. She was too frail. She was... *in need of a chance.*

"Very well, Nettie. I shall take you on for a month's trial."

Nettie's rigid posture sagged and Sophie wondered if she would swoon in her relief.

"Thank you, Mrs. Bennett."

Sophie pulled a sheet of paper from her desk and quickly wrote out a message for the asylum director, then rose from her desk. "I shall send for your belongings and then settle you into the room you will share with the cook once I have hired one."

"You don't need to send a note, ma'am. My things are outside." The subtle darkening of Nettie's cheeks might have been a blush. "Mrs. Yarrow, the ward director, said she'd know you hired me if I didn't come back."

"Then bring your things inside and I shall show you where they go."

Nettie ducked a curtsey and hurried out. The bag she returned with could not have contained more than a single change of clothing. Sophie called herself a fool for allowing her sympathy to rule her actions. First Miss Graham, now Nettie. But the meager contents of that bag made her glad she'd done so.

She led Nettie to the ten-foot square room beside the kitchen. Two recently delivered narrow bed frames resided against opposite walls. Unrolled mattresses and bedding lay stacked in the middle of each until ready for use. Crammed between the beds was a short chest of drawers topped by an earthenware bowl and pitcher for water. Small wooden chests sat at the ends of each bed for personal belongings. Pegs lined the wall beside the door for hanging cloaks and aprons. The floor was bare, but Margery had suggested they make rag rugs for each bedchamber to ease the chill of getting out of bed on cold mornings.

"You may put your belongings away, then come be introduced to Miss Chandler, the housekeeper. She twisted her ankle this morning so is recovering in her room. She will instruct you on your duties and train you for any you need to learn once her ankle is better."

Nettie put her bag into the chest farthest from the door, then turned and followed Sophie through the kitchen toward the hall.

"Should I bring Miss Chandler some tea or make her an onion poultice for her ankle, Ma'am? It will keep the swelling down."

Sophie turned, surprised and pleased that the woman had anticipated the need without being told. "You know how to make one?"

"Yes, Ma'am. I made them lots of times for my uncle when his knees swelled up. If you can spare a bit of salt to go with the onions it will work faster."

Sophie knew nothing about poultices except that Margery had often used them to ease Sophie's pain in the aftermath of her husband's angry tirades. "Use what you need. Put the kettle on for tea as well. Miss Chambers' room is the first door to the right along the hall. Bring them to her room when you've finished." She eyed Nettie's gaunt frame and added, "There is bread in the box and butter in the crock if you are hungry."

"Yes, Ma'am. Thank you." Nettie bobbed a curtsey, then checked the kettle for water. "I'll see to it right away."

Sophie hesitated, wondering if it was wise to leave Nettie alone in the kitchen. The muscles of her shoulders and neck knotted again. She still questioned every idea she had, every opinion she expressed, every decision she made. Before losing her parents Sophie had been confident and sure of herself, but Dalton had scorned Sophie's competence so often that she had ceased trusting her common sense. And the mistake she had made in marrying him proved how wrong her judgement could be.

LADY DALTON'S DECEPTION

The life she now led demanded she make decisions every day and she had gradually begun to believe she was not as useless as he claimed. She did not know if Nettie's story was true, or if she could be trusted, but anyone she hired would be a stranger. She needed staff in order to take on boarders and she must start somewhere.

Reminded of boarders, Sophie wondered what Miss Graham was doing since she'd sent Nettie to her. The noises upstairs had ceased. In fact, it was suspiciously quiet.

Chapter 4

"I don't like her, Uncle Alec."

Startled, Alec looked up to see Janet in the doorway of his kitchen. Though she had only been enrolled for three days, Janet had acquired a better fitting dress. The yellow and cream striped muslin was modest and as fashionable as those worn by the other young ladies he saw around town. The fabric was not one of those he'd supplied for new clothes, so Mrs. Bennett must have altered one of her own dresses until the new dresses could be made. He must thank her for that. So far as he could see, Mrs. Bennett had fulfilled her promise to assist Janet's adjustment to life in Halifax, but Janet's sullen expression made him question his assumptions.

"Why is that?"

"She's too concerned with silly details like who should lead whom to dinner or sit next to whom at the table. According to her, I should know the connections of every person of rank and avoid close connections to anyone who does not conform to what is socially acceptable." She snorted. "I don't believe I am either inferior or superior to anyone else, and I have no intention of acting as though I do."

Alec's brows lowered. He had accepted Mrs. Bennett's suggestion that Janet wait to join the lessons with her other students until she had clothes that fit properly. He hadn't considered that Mrs. Bennett might think Janet inferior to them. "Has she treated you unfairly?"

"Not the way you mean, but she has not allowed me to mix with her other students."

"I thought she explained her reasons for delaying your introductions."

Janet frowned. "It is more than that. I don't think she believes I am smart enough to take lessons with them, but I am. In fact, I do sums better than any of them. I've heard her correct their mistakes. She has them list their allowances and expenditures in a ledger, but doesn't quiz them about figuring the best prices for goods or how to set aside funds for emergencies."

She strode the rest of the way into the kitchen and checked the kettle before poking the firebox underneath. Taking down the tea crock. she measured out a spoonful of leaves, and set out cups, all the while voicing her complaints.

"She won't let me cook anything, but when I left she was interviewing a skinny woman from the Poor Asylum who looked too sick and weak to walk across the room let alone cook or clean for anyone."

Alec leaned back in his chair and folded his arms. So that was it. Janet was used to doing all the household chores on the farm. Obviously, it had not occurred to her that she no longer needed to do chores. "I pay her for your board," he explained. "You do not have to cook your own food."

"But I want to. Miss Chandler doesn't make cornbread or oatcakes. She didn't even know what they were until I told her." She paused, her blue eyes reflecting her indignation.

"I've cooked for Papa ever since we lost Mama, so it isn't as though I don't know how."

"It's not that you don't know how, it's that you don't have to." Alec took the teapot from her and set it on the table, then tugged her down onto the spare chair. "You had to grow up too fast, Janet. I know you and Rory worked together to keep the farm going but now you don't have to work so much. Mrs. Bennett plans for you to join the rest of her students when they return from their class holiday."

"I still don't like her. She smiles when she talks but you can tell she isn't smiling inside. She is too polite. She never laughs."

Alec had to admit Janet had described Mrs. Bennett's pleasant demeanor more accurately than he'd been able to define. It was as though a real smile would expose more than she dared share with anyone. Yet, he had heard her and Miss Chambers laughing together occasionally. And she had not known he watched her from the upstairs window while she giggled and played fetch with the stray dog that resided under her porch until last spring. What went on behind that polite facade?

Janet stood and poured boiling water into the teapot before again taking her seat and folding her arms across her chest. "And when she talks to me she only talks about my lessons or about the rules I have to follow."

Alec heard the hurt and confusion beneath her complaints and had to swallow the shaft of grief that rose. Janet needed comfort but he'd let her down.

The twelve years between his brother and himself had meant Rory had always been bigger, stronger, and better than Alec in every way. Rory wasn't supposed to die. How could Alec be responsible for Janet's happiness and well-being when he could never be the man his brother had been?

Bloody hell.

Mrs. Bennett had not been ready for boarding students. He had imposed on her and let Janet down at the same time. He was ashamed to admit he'd passed his niece to Mrs. Bennett because he wasn't ready to deal with the responsibility. *Had been afraid of the responsibility.* Rory would have been ashamed of him. He was ashamed of himself.

But what else could he have done?

He leveled his gaze on Janet's unhappy expression. "So long as you live with her, she is responsible for you, so you must follow her rules. Many of them weren't important on the farm but are necessary in town."

Janet said nothing, but her gaze bored into his, and her tightly held mouth spoke volumes.

He sighed. "It's early days yet, Janet. You need to give her a chance to know you." He quirked his brow. "Tell me how you spend your time."

Her gaze shifted. "I mostly stay in my room. If I can't do lessons with the other students and I can't do anything useful there's not much point in leaving it."

"Then you spend no time together in the evenings? What about when her classes are finished? Or at mealtimes? Does she make no effort to include you or make you feel at home?"

Janet glanced at him, flushed, and looked away again. "She and Miss Chandler usually sit in the parlor and do needlework while they read aloud to each other if they aren't doing school things or unless Mr. Farnsworth comes to dinner. They have invited me to join them, but don't insist on it."

"But you do not join them. Why not?"

Janet' eyes glistened and their lids reddened. "I don't fit. She and Miss Chandler don't know anything about farming or timber and I don't know anything about dukes or earls or poets or... or anything that interests them. And when Mr. Farnsworth is there I'm supposed to act like a *proper* lady and listen while he talks about mining and England and Napoleon." She straightened her posture and raised her head, her features tight. "So I just go to my room."

Alec knew Farnsworth. He liked the man and knew he'd begun courting Miss Chandler within weeks of his arrival to supervise the timber Alec brokered for the Farnsworth family. John Farnsworth was solid, dependable, and smart, but it wasn't hard to believe his conversation would hold little interest for a fourteen-year-old girl.

"That can't help things much, though, can it?" He rubbed the back of his neck. "Have you tried telling her how you feel and why you spend all your time in your room? She might believe you prefer to be alone and think she is giving you privacy."

Before Janet could respond, a frantic knock on the door interrupted them. The rapid tattoo came again before he could reach the door. His mild irritation at the visitor's impatience turned to alarm when he opened the door.

Mrs. Bennett stood on the back step huddled under a thick shawl that was her only defense against the brisk wind outside. Contrary to her usual impeccable appearance, she wore no hat or gloves. Her pale features reflected disquiet and her voice held a note of panic.

"Is Miss Graham here?"

"Yes, she is."

Relief seemed to melt her bones and she slumped for an instant before she pulled her shawl tighter around her shoulders and recovered her usual composure. He stood aside and gestured for her to enter. "Is that a problem?"

She looked past him toward the kitchen and he assumed she saw Janet sitting at the table. "It wouldn't be had she asked me before leaving. I went to check on her and she was missing." She turned her gaze back to him. "One of the rules for any of my boarders is that no one is to leave the academy without my permission or proper supervision." She turned her eyes back to Janet. "I explained that to Miss Graham the day she arrived."

Alec watched their silent interplay and almost chuckled at the mutual challenge that ignited the air between them. Then he frowned. Janet had broken the rules set for her. A rule he fully agreed with. He frowned at Janet and hardened his voice. "You did not tell Mrs. Bennett you wanted to see me?"

Janet looked down and shook her head.

"Why not?"

"She was busy and I saw you come home." She looked up and confessed. "I didn't think she'd notice."

"I did. It is my job to notice." Grim exasperation coated Mrs. Bennett's tone and Alec had to admire the control she showed his unrepentant niece. "I am responsible for your safety and comfort while you abide with me. I care what happens to you."

Janet rose from the table and sneered, "You don't care about me. You care about Uncle Alec's boarding fees."

"Janet! You will not speak to Mrs. Bennett, or any adult, in such a manner."

Mrs. Bennett flinched and her eyes widened at his harsh tone, but she turned to Janet before he could say more. "While I require your uncle to pay for the cost of housing and feeding you, that doesn't mean I don't care about your safety or whether or not you are happy."

Her stiff posture eased and her voice softened. "I, too, lost my parents and was sent to a boarding school where I felt out of place and lonely." She adjusted her shawl again, and Alec suspected she did so to mask the depth of her emotions. "But there are rules that must be followed in any situation if for no other reason than that we must learn to live with one another." She stopped fussing with the shawl and faced Janet, her expression controlled. "Unless there is a good reason not to, I shall always give you permission to visit your uncle when he is home." Her voice took on a firm, no nonsense tone. "However, you are never to go to his offices on Water Street alone at any time. Beyond the safety factor of knowing where you are, it is a courtesy to request permission and avoid unnecessary worry."

Alec folded his arms over his chest. "You owe Mrs. Bennett an apology, lass."

"I am sorry, Mrs. Bennett." Janet flushed and added, "I truly did not think you would notice. I would have been back before supper."

Mrs. Bennett's lips turned up. "I went to see how you had rearranged your room."

Janet blinked in surprise. "You knew I changed things around?"

"The sound of a bed dragged across the floor over one's head is rather hard to miss." She met Alec's gaze and he noted a rare twinkle of amusement that accompanied her ironic comment.

Alec grinned and Janet brought her hand to her mouth and giggled. "I suppose so."

LADY DALTON'S DECEPTION

"Now that I know where you are, I shall see you at supper." She turned back to the door, then stopped and looked back at Janet. "Would you like to invite your uncle to join us for dinner one evening, Miss Graham?" She looked at Alec. "Perhaps tomorrow, if he has no other plans?"

A jolt of pleasure hit Alec and it wasn't only that dinner would give him time with Janet. Mrs. Bennett had never reached beyond the most basic civilities before this. Her disclosure that she'd been orphaned was the first personal information she had ever shared with anyone that he knew of. Dinner offered him a chance to learn more about the elusive widow.

That unexpected twinkle in her eye gave him hope. What else might she share over time?

Chapter 5

His knock on the door was answered by a wisp of a young woman too frail and tiny to be anyone other than the maid Janet had described the day before. Her gaunt form and the dullness in her dark complexion raised his concern. Swathed in an oversized apron, she nearly disappeared in the folds of cloth. He almost reached out to offer her his arm for support before she curtsied and stepped back for him to enter.

"Mr. Graham, sir. You are expected."

To his surprise, Margery Chandler sat with Mrs. Bennett and Janet in the parlor. Had he mistaken Miss Chandler's position as housekeeper? Staff did not normally join dinner guests.

"I invited Miss Chandler's betrothed, Mr. Farnsworth, to join us for dinner as well," Mrs. Bennett said once he was seated. "I wasn't sure if you would feel comfortable being the only male at the table." Her fingers twitched ever so slightly where they rested in her lap. "You and he do business together, isn't that right?"

Ah-hah. Miss Chandler's marriage to a man of business would raise her place in society. Once married, Miss Chandler would be expected to entertain her husband's business associates and social peers. Did that small twitch mean

Mrs. Bennett was nervous about paving the way for those changes?

"Yes, we do." Alec smiled and bowed to Miss Chandler. "The lumber for his family's mines will be held in my warehouse until shipped to England."

The frail maid carried a tea tray into the room and he again had to fight the urge to relieve her of the burden. When she placed the tray on the low table between Janet and Mrs. Bennett, Janet shifted in her seat but Mrs. Bennett cleared her throat and Janet settled again.

"Thank you, Nettie." She turned to Janet. "Would you like to pour the tea, Miss Graham? You know how your uncle likes it prepared."

Janet raised her eyebrow and flashed him a quick glance before she dripped a dollop of honey into the cup, then filled it with fragrant tea. The eyebrow told him how silly she thought the formality of Mrs. Bennett's suggestion. Still, after serving him, she asked Mrs. Bennett and Miss Chandler how they liked their tea and finally prepared her own.

Nettie announced John Farnsworth moments later. He bowed to the ladies but his cheerful expression faded when he spied Miss Chandler's bandaged foot. "My dear, have you hurt yourself?"

"I made a misstep on the stairs yesterday but it is not serious." She lowered her foot and stood. "It barely twinges now. See?"

Alec bit back a smile when Farnsworth hurried to take her arm and insist that she be seated again. It amused him that a man of normal good sense and canny intelligence lost all dignity in the name of love. Farnsworth doted on Miss Bennett's housekeeper and her blushing response told him the feeling was mutual.

He glanced at Mrs. Bennett. Her eyes glittered with moisture held in check and her smiling lips trembled. Had her late husband been equally solicitous? Did she still grieve for him? Was that why she avoided most social events? Her only interaction seemed to be with Miss Chandler.

It occurred to him that perhaps she would be losing more than a housekeeper when Miss Chambers married and returned to England. The irony of her apparent bond with Miss Chandler struck him anew. Halifax was not London, but rank and station still had their limits. What had altered those boundaries between Mrs. Bennett and Miss Chandler?

Sophie was glad she had suggested Margery invite Mr. Farnsworth to join them tonight. If it had not been for his niece, Sophie would never have invited Mr. Graham to dinner. But she had responded to the lonely defensiveness she recognized in the girl's eyes and acted on impulse.

Sophie remembered the lonely months that followed her own parents' deaths and sympathized. The school was a necessary haven for Miss Graham, but it was not the home the child knew. Nor was it where she wanted to live. Which is why Sophie had spoken without thinking.

Until she married, Sophie had been confident in her ability to set visitors at ease, but her hostess skills had not pleased her husband. Her impulse to speak without carefully assessing whether her courtesies were inconvenient to her husband had been one of her many faults and why her husband had not allowed her to socialize with his friends. He insisted that what she had intended as spontaneous kindness was nothing more than foolish thoughtlessness. At times like this, she feared he'd been right.

Mr. Farnsworth turned to Sophie. "Margery told me that you will take on boarding students and hire more staff. Have you had many applicants?"

"As you can see, I have hired a maid. I will be interviewing additional staff tomorrow." She cleared her throat. "Tell me, Mr. Graham, do you know anyone who would make a good man of all work and who could also act as watchman? I am sure most families would prefer someone of appropriate presence to guard the premises, yet I am not sure where to start looking or who might offer reliable references."

She glanced in Mr. Graham's direction and her breath caught when fissures of heat shot up and down her torso. His warm gaze met hers and reminded her he believed she was a widow.

Worse, when in his presence, she wished it were true.

He blinked as though her question changed the direction of his thoughts. "I may. I employ watchmen at the warehouse as well as a few who maintain the building. I shall inquire of them and, if you like, do a preliminary interview before sending them to your door."

"That would be most kind."

Mindful that her intent for the evening had been for Janet to feel more at home, Sophie turned to her. "When I've finished with my interviews perhaps you might like to visit the seamstress again to look at fashion plates for the lovely new fabrics your uncle brought you. Since there will be no classes, I am free to escort you."

They finished their meal and removed to the drawing room where Mr. Farnsworth made sure Margery rested her foot on the stool again. Janet took a seat beside her uncle who asked her if she liked the fabrics he'd provided. Sophie settled into her usual chair beside the hearth, happy to let the others converse with one another.

A moment later Margery gasped. "So soon?"

Sophie turned to see Margery's hand at her throat, her face pale, and her eyes wide as she stared at her betrothed. He leaned forward and grasped her other hand.

"We would have the safety of a convoy to bypass the American blockades."

Sophie's breath caught. Did he plan for them to leave before spring as originally planned? *How soon?*

"The captain assures me it will be safer than waiting since the blockades are likely to become more numerous and dangerous if matters escalate." His voice lowered and she was unable to distinguish his words, but Margery's flushed cheeks made Sophie suspect he'd suggested other benefits of moving their marriage date forward. He took Margery's hand in his. "If we book passage with him I must do so soon or others may claim the cabin space he offers."

Margery broke her gaze from his and turned to Sophie. "Mr. Farnsworth has learned of accommodations to England aboard a ship returning to England next month."

Sophie's throat dried and she swallowed hard and echoed Margery's words. "So soon?" She had struggled to accept losing her friend come spring. But November? It was *too* soon. Yet would the time ever feel right?

Sophie saw Margery's guilt at leaving so quickly, as well as her desire to agree with Mr. Farnsworth's plan. After all Margery had done for her when Sophie was hurt and afraid, could she let her selfish emotions interfere with Margery's happiness? If Margery faced danger from increased blockades, Sophie would never forgive herself. She blinked when tears stung her eyes.

She forced a smile. "Is there time to call the banns? What day must you leave?"

Margery's shock-frozen posture eased and she turned back to Mr. Farnsworth.

His tension also eased and his voice cheered. "If the banns are called this Sunday and we marry the day after the third call there will be time." He hesitated, then stroked Margery's hand again and added, "That is, if you approve."

Margery darted an apologetic glance at Sophie who made herself smile encouragement. Margery turned back to Mr. Farnsworth and nodded her agreement.

Sophie smoothed her skirts and strove for a light tone. "Then we've a wedding to plan and but a short time to do so."

"A *wedding*?" Miss Graham looked away from her uncle to join in the conversation. "Will you have a new dress made, Miss Chandler? Uncle Alec has brought me so many pretty fabrics I am sure he would not mind if I passed one of them to you." Then she clapped her hands over her mouth. "Oh, forgive me, I should not have interrupted."

"Our conversation was not exactly private, though if this were a formal party it would be best to make your offer in private and only after speaking to your uncle. However," she added to soften her rebuke, "such an offer is quite generous and good hearted of you."

Mr. Graham reached out and took his niece's hand. "If Janet wishes to make a wedding gift to Miss Chandler and no one else objects, I see no reason why she should not do so. For that matter, all three of you could come to the warehouse where Miss Chandler might select one to her own taste. It would still be Janet's gift to you."

"Oh, yes. I should like that above all else." Miss Graham turned to Sophie, and her eyes sparkled with excitement. "We could all look at the fashion plates."

Margery sent Sophie a wide-eyed look that mirrored Sophie's own astonishment at Miss Graham's enthusiasm and her uncle's generous offer. It was the first time the girl had shown more interest than civility required for anything since she had arrived. Her delight amazed Sophie after witnessing her sullen outburst the day before. She had not shown this much interest in her own new clothes.

The doting expression that lit Mr. Graham's eyes when he looked at his niece did odd things to Sophie's heartbeat. How fortunate for Miss Graham that she still had her uncle to care about her. He looked away from Janet and met Sophie's gaze. The warmth there altered to a more intense and entirely different kind of heat, and Sophie's heart beat faster. Early on, when they had first been introduced, he had invited her to attend an occasional play but she had declined his invitation. He had stopped offering to escort her once she made it clear she was not interested in more than casual acquaintance with him or any other gentlemen.

Still, every once in a while, she caught that flash of restrained desire in his gaze and her heart raced no matter how hard she tried to ignore her reaction. That smoldering glimpse told her he found her attractive, something she craved even though she had no right to enjoy the interest of a man who was not her husband. Much as she wished otherwise, she was tied for life to the man she'd fled. Wishing otherwise would not change that, nor did it allow her to betray her vows.

Still, a flash of longing washed through her and she shifted in her chair. She had found pleasure in marital intimacy before what had been tender turned violent. What would it be like to experience that pleasure again? Heat warmed her cheeks and she bit her lips.

Dear heavens!

She blinked, cleared her throat, and turned to Margery with a strained smile. "Fashion plates and imported fabrics! Won't that be fun?"

Chapter 6

Nettie's plight had inspired Sophie to suggest her students take up the Poor Asylum as a Christmas season charity project, but when Sophie surveyed the chaos of old clothing, paper cutouts and glue pots that littered her upstairs classroom a week later, she feared Dalton had been right to scorn her impulsive nature. She had not realized the degree of mess that six young ladies could make with glue-dipped strips of newsprint paper. The small *paper-mache* boxes were sure to be appreciated by people who had no private quarters and few possessions, but wet wheat paste seemed to find its way everywhere.

Despite the mess they created, the girls had worked hard to complete the project with far fewer arguments than she had expected and she was pleased with their efforts. The temporary inconvenience would benefit the asylum and make her students grateful for their own blessings.

Nettie stepped into the room with a broom in one hand and a basket in the other. "Mr. and Mrs. Endicott are downstairs and want to enroll their daughter as a boarding student."

Sophie appreciated the maid's quiet industriousness and was glad she'd taken the chance of hiring her. Good food and adequate rest had already improved her dull, dry hair and complexion. Replacing Nettie's worn and ill-fitting dress with two new sturdy cottons of indigo blue made her look less gaunt and, though still rail thin, she no longer looked sickly.

Nettie's improved appearance removed Sophie's concern about the validity of Dalton's disdainful criticism. Certainly, her decision to hire Nettie despite her misgivings had proved to be one she did not regret. The young woman had adapted quickly to her duties and rarely needed direction.

"Thank you, Nettie." Sophie gestured to the room as she passed the maid. "It seems the girls decided to make Japanned keepsake boxes for the Poor Asylum residents. You will need to scrub the tables before the Ladies' Auxiliary meets tomorrow. We don't want glue on the sewing projects."

Nettie held up the basket. "Yes, Ma'am, I'll put the scraps in here, then clean the tables."

Downstairs, Sophie greeted the Endicotts. The pretty matron and her daughter looked very much alike, though Mrs. Endicott's figure was plump while her daughter's was still coltishly slender. Light brown curls peeped out from under both their bonnets, and two pairs of dark brown eyes turned to Sophie when she entered the room.

The man who stood when she entered wore the uniform of an army officer and had the look of a someone whose fondness for spirits had turned his nose and cheeks permanently pink and his middle slightly soft. His gaze, however, was direct and as clear as those of his wife and daughter.

"Good afternoon. I understand you wish to enroll Miss Endicott as a boarding student?"

Mrs. Endicott nodded, but it was her husband who answered. "I am being transferred further inland and my wife intends to go with me. We believe camp life is no longer appropriate for our daughter, however. When I saw that you were to take in boarding students I asked around and was impressed with what I heard about you and the Academy. I decided your school would be the best solution for all of us."

Sophie glanced at the girl and was relieved to see she did not appear to be unhappy with her father's decision. She moved to her desk and removed a set of the papers she'd had printed for the families of her students. "You should look over the rules, curriculum, and fees before filling out the enrollment information." She turned to his wife and daughter. "While your husband reviews everything, would you like to see the rooms? Only one is taken so you may choose from the others."

A half hour later, the Endicotts took their leave and Sophie had her second boarding student. By the end of the week, she had two more. Miss Caroline Hawthorne was a shy girl from a community just north of Halifax whose relatives hoped she would become more outgoing in a boarding school. Miss Georgina Wilkes was an exuberant girl whose parents hoped Sophie could tame into acceptable demeanor. She and Miss Graham bonded immediately.

She also acquired the rest of her staff. Mr. Graham sent the brother of one of his employees to her within days of her request. Jamie Pike now resided over the empty stable at the back of the Academy property. Bess Delaney had immediately taken over as housekeeper so Margery could prepare for her wedding and subsequent return to England. Best of all, Sophie decided, the Endicotts' former cook, Hester Babcock, had not wished to leave Halifax and now reigned over the Academy kitchen. So long as she maintained her enrollment of both day and boarding students she would be able to support herself and her growing staff.

The day of Margery's wedding dawned cool but free of rain or snow. Since flowers were out of season, Miss Graham had arranged clusters of ivy and holly tied with red twine for the alter. Sophie thought the bright red holly berries offered cheerful color to the occasion.

It also pleased her to see several of their fellow parishioners had come to the church. The low hum of conversation ceased when the vicar and Mr. Farnsworth, with Mr. Graham as their first witness, entered and took their places at the front of the alter.

Sophie waited in the foyer with Margery who had chosen a soft pink wool for her dress. When the vicar signaled he was ready, Sophie preceded Margery down the aisle where she took her place as second witness.

The vicar spoke of marriage as a solemn promise to one another before formally having Margery and Mr. Farnsworth recite their vows. Mr. Farnsworth's voice held a note of tender pledge and Margery's held no hesitation. Sophie's eyes filled with happy tears to see their love for each other.

Their vows spoken, the vicar declared them man and wife, then led them to the side room where the bride and groom signed the church register. Sophie licked her lips when it was her turn to sign. She and Margery had discussed this moment and Sophie had practiced writing her name so that her intentional illegibility might be blamed on a faulty tip.

She would not put the legality of Margery's marriage in jeopardy by using a false name. Her hand shook as she formed the *L* then cramped the rest of the letters so that they could be mistaken for Laurel instead of *Lady* so long as no one expected it to be anything else. She did the same when she wrote Sophronia. Then, when she formed the letters for Dalton, she wrote quickly and at the same time pretended to sneeze. A blotch of ink splattered onto the page so that the letters smeared. "Oh!"

The vicar chuckled. "Not to worry Mrs. Bennett." He sprinkled sand over the page, then shook the excess from the book before putting it back on the table and handing Alec the quill. "You are not the first to blot the page." He smiled. "So long as we are witness to your signing just as you are witness to the marriage, all is well."

She and Margery exchanged relieved glances before Mr. Farnsworth led them out of the chapel where well-wishers cheered the couple as they came into sight. Mr. Farnsworth had reserved the private dining room for a small wedding breakfast along with the room at the hotel in which he and Margery would spend their wedding night.

It wasn't until Sophie was back at the Academy that she faced the stark truth. Writing her name in the registry had disturbed her greatly. Telling people she was Mrs. Bennett did not make it so. But she was no longer the broken-spirited woman she had been as Lady Dalton, either. Her last ties with that life would sail away tomorrow.

Now that Margery was married, Sophie was truly on her own for the first time in her life. Her parents, her guardians, then Dalton had guided and controlled her every action and thought. Miss Longborough had pushed her to agree to leave, and the duke arranged for her escape. Even Margery, dear loyal Margery, had been the one to suggest she open the school and who supported her when in doubt.

What now? Her body hollowed and goose flesh rose along her arms. Was she capable of surviving without anyone to guide her? Dalton had convinced her she could not... *but...*

She owned and ran a school.

She had a satisfactory roster of both day and boarding students.

Her curriculum prepared those young women to be wives to diplomats and town leaders.

Sophie no longer felt like the broken, frightened woman she had been when she arrived in Halifax. She still doubted everything she did, every decision she made. But she made them. She had no choice.

She took a deep breath. She would not allow doubts to destroy the fragile courage that had grown in place of her fears. She blew out the candle, pulled her blankets up to her chin, and shivered with grim determination. Dalton would be livid if he knew she thrived without him.

The nightmare of Dalton in full fury brought her from sleep in a sudden surge of gasped breath and shaking limbs. Once awake, she willed herself to relax, reminded herself she was safe, that he did not know where to find her. She lay in the dark for a long time before she eventually drifted back into sleep. When she did, the nightmares shifted to equally disturbing dreams of standing alone, shivering in a cold, snow-covered lot wearing nothing but her shift while people strode past as though she was not there.

Sometime before dawn, she gave up the effort and rose to dress for the day. Her nightmares were nothing more than the insecurities from her past. She would manage the school on her own and Mr. Farnsworth would make Margery happy. This evening she would bid them farewell and begin anew...again.

In her office, Sophie took out a sheet of paper and sharpened her pen nib. There was so much she wanted to say to Margery, so much to thank her for, so many good wishes she wanted to give her but had been unable to put into words while they prepared for the wedding. Then there was Miss Longborough. She hadn't dared send her news of her arrival or of her improved life lest somehow Dalton learned of it. But she wanted the young woman to know how very grateful she was for the help she and the duke had provided. She wrote what was in her heart to both women. Finally, she wrote a formal thank you to the Duke of Wolverton who had allowed Miss Longborough to convince him of her need, though she knew how much he disliked scandal of any sort.

A soft mist filled the early evening air when Sophie reached the wharf where Margery and her new husband said goodbye to those who'd come to see them off. The setting sun lit a rainbow that Sophie chose to see as an omen of good fortune for their future. The ship would leave the harbor in the small hours of the morning and they would be at sea long before Sophie woke.

A bell sounded from the ship and the captain announced that they must say their last farewells and seek their quarters on board. Margery turned to Sophie, tears glistening in her eyes though she glowed with happiness and love.

"I shall write you often and keep you apprised of everything." She hugged Sophie and whispered, "And let you know if anyone still searches for you."

Sophie hugged her in return, then stepped back, dabbed her eyes and cleared her throat of the emotions clogged there. "Before you go, there is one more thing I must ask of you. Would you see that these are sent to London once you arrive?" She handed Margery letters for the duke and Miss Longborough. She held up the third letter. "This one is for you. Please do not open it until you reach England. There is so much I wanted to say, but could only write."

Margery's eyes filled again though she gave a wobbly chuckle. "I felt the same way." She reached into her reticule and pulled out a folded sheet of paper. "You must not open yours until the ship has left port."

They both laughed as the tears spilled over and they gave each other another fierce hug. Then Margery and her husband strode up the gangplank and Sophie made herself stand and wave gaily before turning to walk away from the only true friend she had ever had.

"Farnsworth will take good care of her, Mrs. Bennett."

Sophie stopped abruptly, disconcerted to see Mr. Graham at her side.

"I know, but I shall miss her terribly." She didn't need his reassurance. Margery had good instincts and had made a good match. She would find happiness with her husband. Nor did she want Mr. Graham to escort her home, though it was clear he intended to do so. She needed to avoid the temptation to seek support from others. Especially the man she suspected was all she had ever wished Dalton to be. Her stomach churned. She couldn't deal with his presence when she felt so vulnerable.

"Do you think you will ever return to England yourself?"

Sophie stomach clenched. "No. I prefer the life I have made for myself here." Her recent vivid nightmares assured her of that. "My school gives me purpose and keeps me busy." She looked away and smoothed her skirt. "I am content."

A dockworker strode past them, his back bent under the load of a duffle bag, and she stepped out of his path to continue away from the dock. Her pulse jerked when Mr. Graham joined her.

"Content?" His voice held a teasing note. "Contentment is for old age, Mrs. Bennett. What of challenge, curiosity, or passion? You are a young woman who dared to cross an ocean to make a new life for herself. How can you settle into the quietude of contentment after taking such a chance?"

A spurt of irritation made her voice tart. "Very easily, Mr. Graham. Teaching volatile young ladies is an adventure in itself. One never knows what crisis one of them will decide afflicts them next. And now that four of them are in residence, there is rarely an hour of the quietude you imagine."

That made him laugh.

His laugh made her flush.

His laugh made her uncomfortably aware of passions that must be caged in the quietude of determined contentment.

Chapter 7

Alec grinned as he fit his steps to those of Mrs. Bennett. "They certainly seem to be a lively group."

The lady had a wry sense of humor that he was only recently aware of. He should be ashamed that he used his niece as an excuse to spend more time in Mrs. Bennett's company, but he'd be lying to himself if he didn't admit that he did. Now that Janet had settled in with the school, he didn't worry about her. She didn't need any more lengths of cloth or frilly-bobs like ribbons and lace either. But he'd learned that if he brought his offerings at half-past ten each morning he could catch Mrs. Bennett when she was between lessons and her students were engaged in journal entries that allowed him time to visit with her over a pot of tea.

He looked forward to her dryly-humorous outlook now that he spoke with her each day. He could also read subtleties in emotions that she often held in check. At the moment, she strove to appear at peace with her friend's parting, but she had twisted the cords of her reticule until they pulled tight against her delicate fingers. It made him glad he'd come to the wharf so she would not feel alone when the newlyweds boarded the ship and disappeared from sight.

Did she think he'd merely come to say farewell to his customer? Despite the tortured reticule cords, he knew she would not like his assumption that she needed support. He did not intend to take advantage of her distressed emotions but neither could he deny he hoped she would allow a less formal friendship to evolve.

Whether or not she admitted it, he'd recently concluded Mrs. Bennett was not as disinterested in him as she'd have him believe. Sometimes she gazed at him with an arrested look of fascination, then fussed with her fingertips like she might be holding herself back from reaching out to him. When that happened, she blushed before looking away and stood straighter, as though erect posture created a wall between them. He would find it amusing except then her mouth always tightened and her eyes looked bleak.

They were bleak now despite her wry response. Something had created deep pools of sadness below her determined reserve, and it was more than the loss of her housekeeper. Hoping to ease her sadness, he searched for a topic that would take her mind from the companionship that would sail with the tide. "Janet says she likes your school better since she has undertaken Christmas projects for the residents of the Poor Asylum."

She nodded. "Nettie spent a week at the asylum when she couldn't find the cousin she was to live with, so Miss Graham and the other students understand that not all are to blame for their circumstances."

Always Miss Graham, not Janet.

He cleared his throat. "I know you maintain formality in the classroom as part of your curriculum of polite behavior, but you need not be so formal when discussing Janet with me. You may call her by her given name when speaking to me. No one ever addressed her as Miss Graham before she came to Halifax, and she says it makes her feel as though she has taken on a secret identity."

Beside him, Mrs. Bennett sucked in a breath and clenched her reticule tighter. "Formal address is something to which she should become accustomed. Casual use of her given name shows a lack of respect." She eased her grip on the twisted strings. "She will soon be of age to be courted, and as such, should expect and demand the esteem it implies. I will not allow any of my students to be treated with anything less than respect."

Why would his suggestion make her defensive? "Casual address is a token of friendship as much as a trespass of social distance. Has someone maligned the privilege of your name in the past? Is that why you are so cautious now?"

Her hand jerked, then released when she turned her cool gaze at him. "We are discussing social behavior, Mr. Graham, nothing personal."

"I see your point and I beg your pardon for trespassing. However, we are discussing my niece and I prefer to speak frankly rather than formally."

"Very well, Mr. Graham." Her lips twitched. "I confess Janet is of a less than formal personality. Though I shall encourage her to embrace the advantageous aspects of formal address so it does not feel so strange and unfamiliar."

He grinned at her diplomatic description of Janet's impatience with formal society. "Since she has little experience in social interaction, perhaps it would be wise to take her to a venue where she can observe such things in reality rather than theory. Would you consider attending a public entertainment with us? You could quietly point out examples as they occur."

Had her hand not rested on his arm as he guided her along the wharf he would not have guessed that his suggestion disturbed her in some way. Yet it had. Her hand had tensed, and her amused smile faltered. As a widow, did she worry that he would have expectations if she let down her guard? Had someone abused the privilege of her good name? Had someone taken advantage of her widowhood at some point? Was that why she had declined all offers of male escort over the past two years?

The idea that anyone would presume on the petite woman perturbed him. Despite his attraction when they met, he had respected her independence once he realized she avoided masculine entanglements in her life. He had been careful to keep his conversation free of familiar innuendo. He still wanted her company, but he hoped to assure her that he would not impose, either. His conscience nagged that he was using Janet and her unpolished view of the world as an excuse to do exactly that. Still, he couldn't quite dismiss the occasional flashes of desire he recognized in Mrs. Bennett's gaze.

He glanced down at her. "I have been invited to a musical evening on Friday evening and am assured I may bring a guest or two."

Startled blue eyes met his and he saw that flash of awareness that brought his own desires to the fore. She blinked and looked away. After a moment she looked back. The fire had been quenched, but there was question in her gaze. "You do not need me to do that."

"But you will be able to point out the subtle ways in which ladies accept or rebuff both men and women from their circle. I confess I do not always know exactly how it is accomplished, only that the signal is received."

They walked in silence for a few minutes before she spoke.

"Very well. I shall come with you and Janet."

Sophie smoothed the deep green velvet of her evening dress and wondered if she had made a mistake in agreeing to attend the musical evening with Mr. Graham. She had been careful to explain to Janet the reason for formality between all but family and close friends. She told herself, and explained to Janet, her goal in taking part was to point out the subtle undercurrents that made formal manners so important in public. But Sophie knew that had not been her true reason for accepting the invitation. She enjoyed Mr. Graham's attentions even though she knew she had no right to enjoy them under the guise of her duties as his niece's headmistress.

Irrational as it was for her to desire a liaison that could never come to fruition, she had agreed because she desired Mr. Graham's company. His frequent arrivals with trinkets for Janet had reawakened the sense of herself that Dalton had crushed. Alec Graham made her feel worthy of respect, and though he sometimes teased, he did not mock. He amused her and made her want to laugh when he told outrageous stories of his youth. He asked her opinion on more than his niece's needs. She did not feel stupid or incompetent when they chatted over tea.

And he is lovely to look at.

She stepped out into the hall just as Janet came down the stairs. Too young for evening dress, she nonetheless wore a pretty blue dress trimmed with tatted lace. Satin ribbons the same color secured her braids. She fairly glowed, and Sophie felt her spirits rise to match Janet's excitement.

The other girls followed with cheerful wishes for a good time. They would be under the care and supervision of Mrs. Delany for the evening while they worked on the last of their knitted projects for the Poor Asylum. Mrs. Babcock had promised to make hot cocoa and biscuits to make their exclusion less disappointing.

The knock at the door sent Sophie's heart racing but she resisted the urge to check that her hair was neatly in place. Mr. Graham was not here for her. He was escorting his niece and Sophie was merely guiding the girl in social behavior.

When he stepped inside, Sophie's throat dried. *Oh, yes, he was very lovely to look at.* Formal evening attire suited his tall muscular shoulders, lean hips, and long legs. Had he trimmed his hair too?

"Good evening, ladies. How lovely you both look."

Janet grinned. "So do you, Uncle. I've never seen you look so dandified."

"You have only seen me at the farm or dressed for business. I am escorting two ladies to a social evening, and I always dress appropriately on such occasions." He took the winter cloak Nettie held and set it around Sophie's shoulders, then did the same for Janet. He offered his arm to each of them. "Let us venture into the world of those stuffy formal manners you complain about so you can see how often they rescue us from awkward situations and intrusive individuals."

Outside, a myriad of stars shone bright in the frigid clear sky. Wood smoke scented the air as they made their way to the carriage. Though their destination was not far, Sophie appreciated the thick wool lap rug Mr. Graham spread across their knees before taking the reins in hand.

Janet chattered happily the entire way and her excitement and curiosity made Sophie smile. Janet had revealed that the isolation of the Graham family farm had been mitigated by evenings of violin and song. Her papa's violin had been left behind in her trek to Halifax, but now that she joined her fellow boarding students in the parlor each evening, she had often cajoled them into singing. The girl had a lovely soprano voice and a wide repertoire of song.

When they reached the Jasper home, Sophie was relieved to see that most of Mrs. Jasper's large family of brothers and sisters, including her fourteen-year-old sister Eleanor, attended. This then, was as much a family gathering as a social evening. Many of the upper families of Halifax were related by marriage, and several of them were also in attendance.

Most of the matrons who greeted her were members of the Ladies' Auxiliary, so Sophie did not feel quite so out of place as she had feared. Nor did she note more than one or two raised eyebrows when Mr. Graham assisted her from the carriage. Janet's presence seemed to satisfy them that she attended for her student's sake since she normally limited her social activities to church functions or the rare assembly dance when Margery had talked her into going.

"I am so glad your uncle allowed you to attend." Mrs. Jasper greeted Janet with a broad smile, then gestured to a girl who stood nearby. "May I make known to you my youngest sister, Eleanor? I believe you are of similar age." The girls acknowledged one another and Eleanor led her away to introduce Janet to the few other young people clustered together at the far wall. Mrs. Jasper turned and flickered an interested glance between Sophie and Mr. Graham.

"And how kind of you to accompany her, Mrs. Bennett. We do not often see you at evening events."

Sophie knew that look. Mrs. Jasper was assessing whether or not Sophie's presence was more than a headmistress supervising her charge. Alec Graham was an eligible bachelor and she was believed to be an equally eligible widow. "Miss Graham is a bit young for evening entertainments, and she has also led a rather isolated life. Her uncle felt she would benefit from my support and guidance. I did not know there would be other young people with whom she might mingle."

Mrs. Jasper's speculative expression faded though her warm welcome remained. "Nonetheless, Mrs. Bennett, I am happy you came."

They soon took their places in the assortment of chairs that had been arranged in several rows from the front parlor to the open doorway connecting what at other times was clearly a private sitting room. At the far end of the room, she spied two musicians with violins, one with a flute, and another sorting music sheets at a pianoforte. A brunette in a sapphire blue satin gown stood in quiet conversation with the vicar. The violinists finished tuning their instruments and Mrs. Jasper directed everyone to their seats so the entertainment could begin.

Janet rejoined them and Sophie noted with amusement that she frequently sent her gaze in the direction of Eleanor's older brother. Mr. Graham did too, and when the young man glanced at his niece, her uncle lowered his brows and scowled. Young Mr. Halibarton quickly directed his attention to straightening the cuffs on his shirt.

Sophie's lips twitched and she murmured, "And you claim you do not know how one discourages unwanted attention without making a scene?"

He shot another glance at the boy. "I said I did not know how others did it."

Chapter 8

The quartet began playing and Sophie's attention switched to the young woman in blue who sang a newly popular song. That was followed by an instrumental piece and a traditional ballad. At the end of the hour, the musicians were granted a break while the guests circulated and enjoyed refreshments.

"Papa played the violin better than the man in the brown coat," Janet commented to Sophie after Mr. Graham excused himself to fetch them each a glass of apple cider. Her eyes shimmered. "I wish I could have brought his violin with me.

"Do you play?"

"Some, but mostly I sang along while he played."

"It was more like he played along while you sang." Mr. Graham rejoined them and handed them each a glass. His expression was one of amused indulgence. "Janet always had a song to sing, even when she was doing her chores."

"She still does," Sophie assured him. "And she often leads the other girls for entertainment in the evening. She has a pleasing voice."

Janet flushed. "Singing was always more fun when the chores were done and Papa played."

"Most things are more fun when the chores are done," Sophie agreed.

LADY DALTON'S DECEPTION

They took their seats again but before the music began, Sophie asked Janet, "What have you observed about the introductions and greetings among the guests so far?"

Janet gazed around the room as though gathering her thoughts. "Those who were well acquainted called each other by their given names but referred to them to others by their rank or surnames. People who didn't know each other well only used surnames." Her lips tightened. "Except everyone introduced me or Eleanor or her brother by our given names because we are still considered children."

"Exactly." Sophie nodded her approval. "Formal introduction and greeting allows you to set the boundary of your interactions. You should be the one who decides if someone may be so familiar as to use your given name. It is a privilege to be bestowed, not one to be taken."

"In that case, I should like you to call me Janet in private but introduce me to others as Miss Graham."

Sophie laughed. "I shall be happy to do so."

Her uncle chuckled and a teasing warmth lit his expression when he told Sophie, "And I would be honored if you called me Alec."

His eyes met hers and she saw the invitation, the hint of attraction, and the question his offer made. Sophie's pulse leapt and panic robbed her of breath. If she accepted his request, she automatically granted him the same privilege. It was something that she would dearly like to do, especially now that Margery was gone and she had no other close friends.

Alec instead of *Mr. Graham*. It need not involve more.

But she had never called any man by his given name. Not even her husband, though she knew from their marriage vows his name was Albert. But she had always called him by his title, and he had never suggested she do otherwise. In return, he had called her Sophronia.

Other than in the family Bible, no one else had used her full name. The introductory letters His Grace had provided for her when she left England listed her name as Laurel Bennett to prevent Dalton from tracing her destination. She had made a place for herself as Mrs. Bennett and was glad to leave Dalton's name in England. It had been two years since she escaped. She no longer feared she was in danger of discovery. And she did not want Alec Graham to call her Laurel.

She was not Sophronia, either.

She was Sophie. Just *Sophie*.

If she denied him the privilege of shared personal names, the pleasant association they had formed over the past few weeks would end. She liked those visits too much. Yet, she should not encourage such a friendship. She was still married even if she wished it were not so.

I should not want him to use my true name.

But she did.

She met his gaze and saw his discomfort at her hesitation. She was taking too long to sort her thoughts. She wanted to have him say her name.

She bit her lip, then blurted, "You may call me Sophie." Hard won caution sent a cold shiver down her spine and she thought of a reasonable explanation should anyone remember her letters of introduction. "My full name is Laurel Sophronia, but my mother was also Laurel, so I have always been Sophie."

His expression lightened again and Sophie's face heated until the tips of her ears burned. She told herself her blush resulted from her fabrication and not his appreciative expression.

Janet watched their conversation with wide-eyed interest and Sophie knew she had to take control of herself and the situation. She turned her focus to Janet. "But he may only do so when there is no one else in hearing lest they assume there is more familiarity between us than exists. A lady's reputation can be put into question if she is too casual with the privilege."

"And remember," Alec said, "that though she may use your given name, you must respect your elders. She will still be Mrs. Bennett to you."

"But if she grants me permission--"

"You will respect your elders. Period."

Janet sighed but nodded her head. "Yes, Uncle."

At the front of the room, the musicians struck a beginning note and Sophie was glad to turn her attention back to the evening's entertainment lest the conversation become more personal. She glanced at the man beside her and wondered if she had acted rashly when she knew she needed to keep her distance.

Alec. Yes, she liked the sound of that.

Sophie. It fit her. Soft and feminine, but straightforward.

Alec settled back in his chair, pleased that another barrier had been lowered. For a moment, he'd feared she would reject his request, worried that he'd pushed too far when she hesitated. She had definitely retreated when he'd asked her to call him Alec. Yet, brick by brick, he would encourage her to take down the wall she hid behind whenever she saw the interest in his gaze. More than the obvious attraction and desire for a beautiful female, she fascinated him. But something made her wary of his interest.

Did she think he posed a danger to her? Why would that be? He was friendly without pressing his attentions more than she allowed. Everyone in Halifax could vouch for his good character. He was single and she was a widow. There was no impediment to either of them enjoying each other's company over more than tea conversations.

His protective instinct made him want to banish whatever fear made her cautious of him. All this talk about names and reputations struck him as more than simple instruction for a young girl on the cusp of society. Not for the first time, he wondered why Mrs. Bennett-- *Sophie* --had chosen to come to Halifax where she had no connections or family. She made it clear she had no desire to visit England's shores again. Why? Whatever her reasons, he knew he wanted to know more than her given name. He wanted to know *Sophie*.

An hour later they applauded the singer at the end of her final song, then bade farewell to Mr. and Mrs. Jasper. Outside, the night sky was clear, the air frigid, and the ground snow had turned to ice. Janet gasped when the cold air surrounded her. "Forgive my manners, but it is too cold to walk sedately." Then she rushed forward, slipping and sliding until she reached the carriage and clambered in.

Sophie shivered then glanced around at the quickly departing guests. "She is right. Dare we make a skating run for the carriage as well?"

Alec held out his arm to lead Sophie across the road but was surprised when she ignored it and made a tiny leap to land with her feet poised to slide across the ice-crusted ground. It wasn't far and she kept her balance. She reached the carriage before he reacted and followed her lead.

At least he would have followed if he hadn't hit a raised bit of turf that caught his shoe and threw him off balance. He tried to catch himself, but when his other foot came down it slipped on the ice and he ended up on his backside, looking like a fool.

All he could do was lay on the ground and laugh at himself because he might just be one. Only a fool would lose his heart over a woman who could slide across the ice while she kept the world at arm's length.

Alec sat up and waved Sophie and Janet back into the carriage. "Stay there. I am embarrassed, but unhurt." He hauled himself up and walked to the carriage, stepping with caution while he brushed the damp from his clothes.

Once they were finally settled in the carriage and on their way, Janet told them Eleanor had invited her and the other students to join a few of her friends for a skating party the next day. Alec smiled at the irony of her request in the light of his ignominious fall.

"May we go?"

He was startled to see she turned to Sophie before looking to him. That shift threw him as off balance as the ice had moments before. Yet hadn't he told her she was not to leave the academy without Sophie's permission?

"If your uncle permits, I see no reason you may not join the party. However, I hesitate to approve the other young ladies' taking part unless I chaperone. I shall send a note to Eleanor's mother to see if that is agreeable to her."

Janet looked to Alec. "Uncle?"

"You may." He flicked a glance at Sophie. "If the other students also go. I did not miss the covert gazes between you and Eleanor's brother."

The carriage arrived at the school and the lamplight revealed the rose tinted flush that colored her cheeks when she declared, "I was looking at Eleanor, not Robert."

"Perhaps not, but he was looking at you."

Alec chuckled when the pink blossomed to red before he exited the carriage to assist the ladies to the street. "I am confident Mrs. Bennett's presence will ensure that all will be as it should be."

At the door, Janet gave him a quick peck on the cheek before hurrying inside out of the frigid night air. "Thank you, Uncle."

Sophie turned at the doorway. "I thank you, too, Mr. Graham . . . Alec. It was a lovely evening and Janet has made new friends."

"As have I, Sophie." She shot him a guarded look and he smiled. "I enjoy our tea talks."

Her lips twitched. "So do I."

Another of those wary hesitations followed her admission. Was this the same woman who tossed him a teasing challenge before dashing across ice without a backward glance?

She shivered and pulled her cloak tighter. "Would you like a pot of tea, before you go, Alec? It is too cold to stand outside."

He grinned. "I should like that very much."

Sophie stepped back for Alec to enter, then led him to the kitchen. "If you don't mind, we'll have it in here. The room is still warm, and I don't wish to disturb Mrs. Babcock since she and Nettie have retired for the evening and will rise before dawn."

Alec sat at the sturdy work table in the center of the room while Sophie rekindled the fire and set the kettle in the hob to heat. It was a comfortable kitchen. The room had been whitewashed and three aprons hung from pegs on the wall. On the floor by the door was a rag-rug. A hutch beside the fireplace held the tea things. Serving bowls and dinner plates filled the shelves above the hutch.

After assembling the teapot and cups, she sat opposite him while they waited for the water to boil. "I enjoyed the music this evening." Her eyes twinkled and she added, "Even though the gentleman in brown was not up to Janet's standards"

"She was right, though." Alec assured her. "Rory could fiddle to delight the angels on high. Once he heard a tune he could play it without a single missed note, while making it grander or faster, or sweeter than it was played for him in the first place."

"Do you play any instruments?"

"I was better at listening than playing anything, though I did join in with the bodhran when I was a boy."

"What is that?"

"A hand-held drum with a double-sided drumstick for keeping time." Alec smiled to think of the rousing evenings of his childhood. "I have a sense of rhythm, but I can't carry a tune. Rory was the musical one. Between his fiddling and Janet's singing it was better if I just gave them an appreciative audience." Alec leaned back in his chair. "Janet says you teach some of the girls the pianoforte."

"I am moderately competent but I would never cause a fluttering of angels." She stood, then moved to the fireplace and checked the kettle. "I do enjoy playing, though." She wrapped a cloth around the handle and poured the boiling water into the teapot. "I was fortunate to be able to trade lessons in deportment in exchange for the instrument in the drawing room."

They each took a sip of tea and a comfortable silence settled between them. During the day, there was always a murmur of sound drifting down the hall or overhead. Someone was always coming or going or speaking to someone in another room. But now, in the kitchen after an evening surrounded by people and music it was quiet. Relaxed.

Alec noticed Sophie's slender fingers wrapped around the cup and was surprised that she did not wear her wedding ring. He'd never noticed that before. Most women continued to wear their rings as proof of their widowhood, especially when there were children involved. But Sophie had no children.

His grannie claimed widows did not remove their rings unless they wished to form a new attachment. But Sophie had been adamant that she did not seek a new husband, and she had cast no lures as a consenting widow. On the other hand, a cynical barmaid he knew declared she would sell her wedding ring, and good riddance, the instant the devil's spawn she'd married was consigned to hell. When and why had Sophie stopped wearing hers?

What had been idle curiosity grew into a need to know. How long had Sophie been married? How soon after their marriage had her husband been sent to the Peninsula? She had no children, so probably not very long. How soon after his death had she come to Halifax? A sudden thought made him tighten his hand on his cup. *Had she been married at all?* She'd had no family or friends in Halifax before her arrival.

LADY DALTON'S DECEPTION

Had she been banished for a scandalous indiscretion? His thoughts formed words and escaped before he should have stopped them.

"Tell me about your husband. I should not pry, but were you truly married?"

Chapter 9

Sophie choked on her tea and spent the next panicked minute struggling for breath and answers.

Where did that come from?

While they chatted, she had drifted into the half-remembered sense of domestic comfort from her childhood before her parents' untimely deaths. The silence of the house, the scent of Darjeeling tea, and the quiet discussion about Alec's childhood had all lowered her defenses. His question sent her emotions spinning.

She should not have deluded herself into thinking that enough time had passed for her to relax into her new life. She should not have frolicked across the ice outside the Jasper home. She should not have invited Alec in.

"My marriage was legal and very real, Mr. Graham, but my memories of my husband are not for public consumption." She looked down at the table rather than reveal the thin line between truth and lie. She had purposely avoided making up more stories than necessary about the non-existent Mr. Bennett, but how long could she use grief to avoid more lies about her past? "Perhaps we should return to formal address if you believe it gives you the right to my private thoughts." She stood and strode to the door. "It is late and I believe it would be best if you returned home."

LADY DALTON'S DECEPTION

He stood, too. "I beg your forgiveness for upsetting you. I asked because I saw you wear no wedding ring. I did not intend to cast aspersions on your good name, though I shall leave as you wish." He took his coat from the peg on the wall and put it on. "I meant it when I said I enjoyed your friendship. I hope we may remain friends and you will still allow me the privilege of your name. I would like for you to continue to use mine."

Shock made Sophie's heart hammer in her chest. She had enjoyed the evening until he'd shaken her with his question. And it had been so long since anyone had called her by her true name, the name her parents had used and that made her feel loved and cherished. Even Margery had maintained the fiction of her Mrs. Bennett identity.

"I do not wear my ring because it no longer fits." Sophie bit her lip and grasped the fabric of her skirts. "I will not confuse or upset Janet by rescinding the privilege without explanations I prefer not to make, so we shall continue as we began this evening. Perhaps it would be best, however, if we did not take tea together for a few days."

Alec nodded. "Thank you, Sophie. I shall not trespass again, but please know that you may share your thoughts with me without fear of exposure, condemnation, or ridicule."

He opened the door and left without further comment.

Sophie crossed her arms around her waist and leaned against the door once he was gone. She made herself breathe slowly until she calmed her racing pulse. After the first few months of living in Halifax, few had asked her about her past. Since she had claimed that her grief was still too fresh to discuss her husband or his service, her story was easily accepted. No one had questioned the few vague answers she had revealed about her background.

She had not repeated those falsehoods in more than a year.

Finally, she felt calm enough to clear away the tea things, damper the hearth fire, and prepare for bed. It took longer before she settled into a restless sleep filled with more nightmares in which Dalton arrived at her door.

Morning dawned at last, and Sophie rose from her bed, exhausted and heavy-eyed, but grateful for the respite from her night terrors. *Dalton is in England and I am safe in Halifax.*

After the disturbing trauma of her dreams, it seemed strange to move about without pain, despite the images being no more than memory driven visions. The nightmares had lessened in frequency over the past two years, but never in their intensity. The taunts, the pain, the agony of loss remained as strong and frightening as they had been in real life. She lifted her chin and crossed to the vanity.

He can no longer hurt me.

She washed and dressed for the day, then went to her desk to write the note to Eleanor's mother.

At breakfast, four pairs of eyes watched her with barely restrained question when Sophie seated herself at the head of the table. She glanced at Janet, who did not look the least bit sorry that she had so obviously told the other girls about the proposed skating party. "I have sent a note to verify Miss Eleanor's invitation. When I receive an answer, I shall inform you of its contents. In the meantime, after you have finished your meal, I suggest you write your weekly letter to your family."

To everyone's relief, the answer arrived within the hour to assure Sophie that her students were welcome to join the rest of the party and that her added chaperonage would be appreciated. When a carriage arrived to take them to the pond soon after, Sophie resolved to enjoy the unexpected inclusion. She would not let the past ruin her days even if it sometimes ruined her nights.

Alec rose and went to his warehouse shortly after dawn. His breath puffed clouds in the cold and his frustrated thoughts plagued him with recriminations. He had lain in bed for hours before finally drifting into sleep. What kind of dunderhead asked a woman of careful propriety if she had really been married to her husband?

One like me.

He unlocked the office door and crossed the room to start a fire in the iron stove. Clyde followed him in from his night prowling and leapt up onto the desk. He settled with his paws tucked in and let his tail flick before wrapping it around himself then watched Alec strike the tender to the wood.

That done, Alec sat and eyed the ginger cat who stared back without blinking. "I shouldn't have asked such a rude and intrusive question, Clyde."

He replayed the evening they'd spent together. She had been reluctant to grant him permission to call her by her given name. Yet she had surprised him with that flash of playfulness after the snow had turned to ice. What had sparked that carefree change? And who was the woman he'd glimpsed before he'd ruined it all by asking if she had actually been married?

"Something other than surprise made her choke on her tea." Her eyes had filled with panic though she struggled to mask it behind refined affront when she ordered him to leave. Something was wrong if a thoughtless question frightened an upstanding woman of reserve like Sophie. Yes, she had been married. *But something was definitely wrong.*

Who was the fellow she had married? Had she married without family approval? Had she eloped with him? Something somewhere, sometime, had trampled Sophie's spirit. Something made her wary of revealing spontaneous behavior. Had society rebuffed her?

Was that what had panicked her? Was she afraid that word of an impetuous marriage would tarnish her reputation and that of her school? If that was the case, he could understand her embarrassment and concern. But it seemed to him that the example of her apparent lack of family support would serve as a far stronger incentive for young ladies to heed her guidance for correct behavior. They would know she understood their feelings even as she counseled them against rash actions. And he was sure she would.

In the light of Sophie's disfavor, Alec decided it was past time for him to see for himself how things fared at the family farm. He'd wanted Janet well settled and safe before concerning himself with what to do with the property. But now seemed a good time to verify all was well. Janet had told him they had finished winterizing the orchards before Rory's accident, so the trees should be protected until Spring. If nothing else, he would gather items of sentimental value to both of them.

He left at dawn.

Walking into the homestead days later gutted him. Everywhere he looked was a reminder of his brother and the absolute reality that he was gone. Alec did not linger but gathered the few things that mattered. Then he located the McInnis fellow and made sure he knew Janet was under Alec's care and would not be marrying anyone to keep the farm. He was glad to note the fellow seemed to be relieved that Janet was safe with her uncle and was willing to oversee matters at the farm.

When he arrived back in Halifax he wasted no time in seeking Sophia's pardon, though he didn't know if she would be ready to entertain his company. Alec crossed the back lot from his house to the school's kitchen door rather than chance the housekeeper refuse him entrance.

Mrs. Babcock grinned when she opened the door and saw the collection of parcels he carried. "More gee-gaws for Miss Graham?" She stood back for him to enter. "You can wait in the parlor while I let Mrs. Bennett know you are here."

Alec walked into the parlor but remained standing by the window. It was one thing to bypass the housekeeper but he would not assume that he was welcome by taking a seat. Beyond the glass, the snow that had covered the ground when he left had melted and partially dried until only patches of the road were muddy. The sky held few clouds and the temperature had warmed enough to entice people to leave their homes for the fresh air. Inside, muted feminine voices floated down the stairs and from the kitchen.

"Clever of you to use the back door," Sophie's quiet voice made him turn around. She looked tired. Had he caused her to lose sleep with his thoughtless question? She wore a demure, but well-cut amber colored wool dress that reminded him of fall leaves in afternoon sunlight. "You may sit, Alec. I told Mrs. Babcock to bring us tea." She crossed to sit in the seat opposite the one she gestured for him to use near the unlit hearth. "What have you brought Janet this time?"

"Rory's fiddle and her ma's hair combs."

Her eyes rounded.

"Now that Janet is settled, I thought it time to see to the homestead. I brought back a few things of hers and his."

"That must have been difficult." Sympathy softened her voice.

"It had to be done." Alec's throat clogged. He cleared it, then held out the small wooden box he'd found in Rory's dresser. "When we went to the musical I noticed Janet fingering her braids after she saw that Mrs. Jasper's sister wore her hair loose with the sides pulled up. I remembered Rory told me he had set her ma's combs aside for when she was old enough, so I brought them back along with his fiddle."

Sophie opened the box, her mouth softening when she viewed the contents. "They are lovely, Alec." She looked up. "She will be pleased to know you noticed, and that you will allow her to try the style."

"The point of the evening was to show her how town life differs from the country farm. Braids are a staple of practical farm girl's life. Hair combs and ribbons fit town life."

Mrs. Delaney arrived with the tea tray. Sophie poured him a cup and added the dollop of honey he liked before handing him the saucer. When she'd prepared her own, Alec asked, "Are we in charity, Sophie? Am I forgiven for my stupidity?"

Chapter 10

Sophie sipped her tea before answering. She had debated with herself daily since he'd left her kitchen. In retrospect, she realized she had overreacted. He'd not asked about her husband until he saw she did not wear her wedding ring. The question had plagued her, worried her, and tempted her until she'd decided that a glimmer of the truth would explain her reluctance to discuss it and her determination to avoid matrimony in the future.

The heated gleam of interest she'd seen in his eyes so often kept her on edge and raised pointless desires she dared not allow. Would it cool his attraction if he understood? It seemed a fair trade for the tea conversations she looked forward to most days.

"We are." She set her cup down and clasped her hands together in her lap. "And I have concluded that your curiosity is understandable. I do not speak of my husband or marriage because neither were ideal. He was not the man I thought he was and I was not the wife he expected. That is all I am prepared to share, but I hope it explains why I have left off my wedding ring. It no longer fits my life."

She met his gaze and tried to assess his reaction to her admission. His eyes, blue, probing and unblinking, bore into her conscience. She had withheld so much more than she'd revealed. Guilt, then defiant anger washed through her. *Until death us do part.* Marriage to Dalton made it impossible for her to have the life of joy and family she'd dreamed of when she'd had her come-out.

Her heart told her Alec was a kind man of honor who deserved to know that the attraction that sparked their commonplace conversations would never go beyond drawing room visits. Her battered confidence told her she could not trust her heart. Her judgement had been skewed by naive trust when she chose Dalton. It might well be skewed by lonely yearning now.

Alec set his cup down as well, then folded his hands together and sat back in his chair. His mouth pursed. "Mismatched lives often lead to disappointment and I am sorry your marriage did not suit." He studied his folded hands for a moment, then looked up. "But experience tempers our expectations, and you are free of your misalliance. Perhaps it is time for you to let go of your past disappointment and find a new fit." A smile flickered across his lips and his eyes glinted with a teasing light. "Did you enjoy Janet's skating party? Would you like to go skating again?"

Sophie's mouth dried and her heart leapt in answer to that teasing grin. *With you? Oh, yes!* She bit her lip to prevent herself from saying it aloud. "Did you not hear my part of that misalliance? I fell very short of my husband's expectations, just as he fell short of mine." She twisted her fingers together, then smoothed them again when she remembered Dalton sneering at her childish mannerism. "I do not wish to chance the boundaries of matrimony again, nor am I of the nature to be a merry widow." Heat burned her cheeks and she looked away. "I do not think it wise for me to contemplate anything beyond friendship over a pot of tea."

LADY DALTON'S DECEPTION

Had she misinterpreted his suggestion? Was the interest she thought he'd shown been nothing more than her repressed desire to be worthy of a kind man's attention?

"Enjoying more company than a pot of tea together does not require a wedding ring that fits, nor must it involve a slip on the shoulder, Sophie." Sincerity banked the heated gleam of the moment before. "Just come have fun for a change. No one will think less of you for enjoying an hour or two of play. Bring your students. Bring Nettie, Mrs. Delaney and Mrs. Babcock for all I care. It is time you allowed yourself to alter the fit of your life to freedom from disappointment."

Sophie fought the urge to twist her fingers again. She understood his assurance, even his veiled reference to clandestine trysts, but the habit of caution had held her in its grip long before she fled England. Dalton had schooled her well. She had watched her words. She had watched her actions. She had watched herself become the shadow of a woman who dared not attract anyone's attention, least of all her husband's.

A schoolmistress did not attract attention.

So long as her students made progress in the graces and home management skills she taught, she was accepted but not expected to put herself forward. Even then, had it not been a matter of survival she would not have chanced it. The notion of releasing herself from the shadows both intrigued and terrified her.

Sophie struggled with her thoughts, keenly aware that Alec waited for her answer. He didn't shift, or drum his fingers, or use any of the subtle signs of impatience Dalton had employed to intimidate her until she gave in to his demands. Alec's patience made her thoughts spin round and round until her dizzy emotions flew in all directions.

She wanted to play and laugh and glide across an icy pond as she had in her youth. She wanted to be merry. She wanted to spend time with him. She wanted more than a half hour over tea but was afraid of where it could lead. She looked at the quiet man who waited out her thoughts.

I want to kiss him.

Mrs. Delaney sounded the gong that signaled the end of the students' journaling hour and Sophie pulled her thoughts under control. Her stomach churned. Anger grew and a long dormant imp of defiance rose in place of caution. All this thought for a single day of skating? It was just a day of fun. And she had made it clear she would not accept courtship.

"Another afternoon at the pond would please the girls."

"I was not concerned with their pleasure, Sophie, I was asking if *you* would like it."

Sophie swallowed the butterflies that took flight in her middle. Not courtship. Not a ring. Not a slip on the shoulder. *Friendship.* With him. Those piercing blue eyes held hers in their gaze and she could not refuse what she wanted in spite of knowing better than to admit the truth.

"I would like a day of skating, too."

Alec's teasing smile beamed wider.

More flights of butterflies, with goose flesh ripples and burning ears, made her look away. Oh, my. What have I done? *Again.*

A burst of girlish chatter floated down the stairs before being followed by the delicate clatter of youthful feet on the treads.

Alec stood. "Shall we say Saturday afternoon? I shall give Janet her combs and the violin, then return to my office." He bowed before stepping out into the hall to meet his niece at the bottom of the stairs.

When Sophie woke Saturday morning, the freezing weather filled her with unaccustomed anticipation. She was to go skating. *With Alec.* Not *alone* with Alec, but with Alec.

She checked the window. The snow glittered in the early morning sunlight and sent sparkling reflections against the fence posts where they emerged from the foot deep drifts. Uneven cloud cover shifted shadows over the landscape but for the time being did not threaten new snow. It was a perfect day for skating on the local pond.

The chill from outside penetrated the window glass and Sophie shivered. Was she deceiving herself? Could she enjoy his company without risking more? Without compromising her values? She believed he was all she had once hoped Dalton would be and wished she trusted herself to judge accurately.

Caution warned that she should continue the restricted, careful routine she had adopted with her new life. But the girl she had been in her youth cried out that a single day of fun was not too much to ask. Did she dare? Would anyone care?

Sophie turned and crossed the room to the wardrobe all the while telling herself it was silly to worry. There was nothing wrong with taking part in an activity instead of merely observing the enjoyment of others. It had been so long since she had done anything for fun. That was all this was. A day of fun.

At Eleanor's skating party she had acted the sedate chaperone by sitting on a conveniently placed log while her students glided around the pond. Eleanor's mother and sister had visited with her and welcomed her presence among the high spirits of the skaters though they, too had taken turns on the ice. It had been a pleasant day. A good day. But she had envied their fun.

From the wardrobe, she pulled out her warmest woolen dress. She'd tacked the hem up so she would not trip over her skirts. Then she retrieved her half boots along with the new ice skates she'd purchased the day after she accepted Alec's challenge.

She fingered the skate laces and resolved she would not sit on the log and watch everyone else have fun. She had once been a very proficient skater. Could she still glide and twirl and leap?

Janet claimed her uncle was skilled as well.

Gentlemen often lent their support to ladies while they skated across the ice. A fissure of heat lanced through her. No one would take it amiss if Alec encircled her waist as they circled the pond but should she allow him to when she did not need guidance or support on the ice? The image was too enticing for her peace of mind.

Her lips twitched when she remembered his challenge. Did she dare let herself do more than glide sedately around the outer edge of the shore?

Yes, she did.

Alec breathed a sigh of relief when the morning dawned clear and bright, perfect for the proposed day at the pond. A distant cloud haze to the north made him suspect the weather would break by evening but not before they were ready to leave. The snow crunched when they walked to the pond from the carriage and he breathed in the redolent scents of tree resin, moss and damp earth. Birds chirped in the sunlight and cheerful voices called to each other as he neared the pond.

Sophie's students quickly tied on their skates and joined friends who were already on the ice. It amused him when Sophie shooed him back when he'd offered to strap the blades to her boots for her. He suspected she intended to avoid any gossip he might be more than a chaperone.

He recognized the shortened amber wool dress as a favorite of hers. The color suited her blond coloring and warmed her complexion. Her cheeks glowed pink from the cold and her eyes had sparkled on the ride out to the pond. If he didn't know better he would say there was a slightly reckless defiance in her expression. Did that mean she was determined to skate despite her abilities... or simply that she was resolved to skate at all? No matter, he would provide her any support she needed.

"How long has it been since you last skated?"

"Not since I left Mrs. Appleby's Boarding School." She gave a final tug to the leather ties, then sat upright. "Seven... no, eight years ago."

"So long? Don't worry, Sophie. I won't let you fall."

Humor lit her eyes when she stood. "Don't worry, Alec," she assured him, "I won't fall." She stepped onto the ice with a firm toe-push from the pond's edge.

Before he could join her, she gained speed and reached the far side of the pond where there were fewer skaters. She skated with smooth strokes, her rhythm controlled and competent, her balance natural, and her grace enthralling.

He'd expected to guide her around the pond, his arm about her waist while she discovered her balance and the rhythm of their gliding steps. That sparkle in her expression should have told him she did not need his guidance. He seated himself on another log to enjoy the sight of Sophie having fun.

Once she reached the far end of the pond, away from the other skaters, she took a few gliding turns. Then, she looked back across the pond as though checking to be sure she had not attracted attention, and did a short spin. She followed the spin with a series of sedate figures as though verifying she had drawn no attention with her actions.

The shoreline jutted out along the left side of the pond and, after one more look toward the other unobservant skaters, she increased her speed in that direction. Just before she raced out of sight behind the bend of the land, she leapt off the ice and turned to land, gliding backward before continuing around to face forward and glide sedately back into view. Clearly, he was an idiot to have thought she would need his help. She skated back to where Alec waited. He applauded as she glided to his side. "My respects, Ma'am. I am impressed."

She rested her hand at the base of her throat, her breaths coming in short rapid pants. "You don't think anyone else noticed, do you? I've not attempted those tricks since I was a child and wasn't sure I would succeed now." She blushed. "Much as I enjoyed renewing my youthful skating prowess, I shall not challenge my luck further. Instead, I need to catch my breath."

Alec grinned and held out his arm. "I'd be happy to offer my support if you like. But only because you wish to catch your breath, you understand. You obviously do not need me to keep you from falling."

Sophie inclined her head with gracious dignity before returning his grin. "Escort is appreciated even when support is not necessary. Thank you."

The ice beneath his feet should have melted in the warmth of that unrestrained flash of joy. Alec needed to catch his own breath.

The warmth beneath the wool of Alec's coat penetrated the leather of her glove when Sophie placed her hand on Alec's arm. The contact shortened her breath more than her brief exercise on the ice. She did not need his guidance, but to her foolish recklessness, she wanted it. She should not risk speculative talk by skating in tandem with Alec Graham. She told herself she did not need to complicate her life and that she should know better. But she allowed him to guide her around the perimeter of the pond. And allowed herself to bask in the sweet pleasure of his company.

"Why have you waited so long before taking to the ice again, Sophie? I gather you lived in London while your husband was away at war, but I know there are ponds for skating in the parks."

His words brought her back to her senses dampening the good cheer his teasing had raised. "Winter was not always beneficial to my health." Winter weather had tried Dalton's patience and he'd often taken his frustrations out on Sophie. He had, of course, begged her forgiveness each time, but had not reformed.

Alec studied her as though looking for signs of illness. "Do you suffer from asthma or are you susceptible to lung fever?"

"I believe it was more the closeness of remaining indoors during inclement weather." Certainly, the more time Dalton spent at home, the more dissatisfied he became with her failures as his wife. "I have not suffered illness since arriving at Halifax, however, and I greatly enjoyed my turn on the ice. Thank you for suggesting it."

They neared the pond bank and spied Amelia Dowling with a young officer who knelt to attach her skates. Amelia blushed and giggled when he clasped her ankle while he tied the leather bindings to her feet. When he finished, he assisted her to stand, then slipped his arm around her back and took her hand in his. They skated away and Sophie noted that he guided her with the protective care required for a beginner. It amused Sophie that Amelia managed to give the impression that her balance was in danger while moving with grace. The minx had skated quite easily at the party the week before.

They reached the embankment and stepped over to the space Amelia had vacated. Amelia's parents chatted with another couple who were still preparing to skate. The couple looked up when Mrs. Dowling greeted them, and Sophie's stomach shriveled into a knot of shock.

"Lord and Lady Marshburn, may I make known to you Mrs. Bennett who is the headmistress of her Academy for Young Ladies, and Mr. Graham who is the uncle to one of her students?"

Sophie's breath froze and black dots swam into her vision. Every nightmare of the past collided into the disaster of the present as her world shattered. Dalton's closest friend and

Beryl Templeton, daughter of the worst gossip in Mayfair, gaped at her.

She had been discovered.

Chapter 11

"You!" Lord Marshburn curled his lip and pulled his wife away from Sophie. Turning from her to face the Dowlings he announced, "Unfortunately, I was acquainted with this woman in England, and have no desire to renew my association with her." His scornful expression was colder than the pond's ice. "Her name is not Bennett. She is Lady Dalton, though I am not surprised she has assumed a fraudulent name. Her desertion of her husband drove him to suicide."

Sophie recoiled at his condemnation, unable to draw a breath. Her heart pounded against her chest, and dark spots increased and circled her vision, making her blink. Her hand clenched against Alec's arm as she fought to breathe. She mustn't faint. She mustn't panic.

Then Marshburn's accusation sank in. *Suicide*?

Sophie swallowed hard. "Dalton would never take his own life."

"Dalton threw himself from the attic of your former residence a week after you deserted him."

"He wouldn't."

"He did."

Mrs. Dowling looked between the Marshburns and Sophie, her gaze alarmed and her voice bewildered. "Your name is not Bennett?"

LADY DALTON'S DECEPTION

Lady Marshburn looked at Mrs. Dowling and her eyes widened. "You said Miss Dowling attends Mrs. Bennett's Academy for Young Ladies. Is *this* the woman who is responsible for teaching your daughter proper social behavior?" She shot Sophie a look of absolute disgust. "She should be shunned, not paid to corrupt the minds of one's daughters."

Lord Marshburn turned to the Dowlings. "I beg your pardon, but my wife and I must excuse ourselves. Perhaps the stench that currently befouls the air will be gone once we have skated for a while."

They circled a wide path around Sophie and skated to the far side of the pond. Mr. and Mrs. Dowling looked at each other, then turned to skate after them.

Sophie stared after them. *Dalton is dead*?

Marshburn's accusation that Dalton killed himself did not make sense. He was too intent on his personal pursuits to be that affected by her actions. Oher than as a bed partner and the target of his rages, she had had no impact on his life, so why would her actions cause him to take it? It didn't fit, but why would Marshburn lie about such a thing?

She watched the Dowlings rejoin the Marshburns on the far side of the pond where other skaters traced figures in the ice. The Dowlings spoke with Amelia and her escort who turned to gape at Sophie. Her students laughed and challenged each other nearby, unaware of the disaster that loomed before her.

The weather remained clear. The snow still glistened in the sunlight. Yet, her fear that Dalton might one day find her had just been turned upside down. Her mind grappled with the impossible. Dalton could never come after her. He would never reclaim her. She was truly free of him, and had been for the entire time she'd lived in Halifax. It couldn't be true. But, according to Dalton's best friend, it was. Numbing shock left her in a daze.

She would not be anonymous Mrs. Bennett now that Marshburn had revealed her secret. She would be the notorious Lady Dalton again. She wanted to cry. But she wouldn't. Not now. Not here. Not--

"You left your husband."

She'd forgotten Alec stood next to her. "Yes."

"You lied about being a widow."

His voice held that flat note that came with disapproval and offended propriety. She blinked back the tears. "Apparently not, though I thought I did. For that, I am sorry." She sat on the log and began removing her skates. "I am not, however, sorry I left him."

Alec's gut clenched and cold disillusion chilled the warmth of their earlier teasing. Sophie's calm statement held no regret, no excuses, no emotion at all. He had admired this woman for two years but she was not who or what he thought she was. He had believed her reserve to be that of a woman who had remained loyal to her husband's memory even though she admitted their marriage had not been ideal. Yet, when accused of abandoning those vows, of deceiving the people who had believed her lies, she didn't deny it. Worse, she confirmed it. How he could have been so mistaken in his impression of her?

He absorbed the appalling realization that he'd been duped. Indignity burned away the chill and left him seething with betrayed anger. He waited for her to say more, but she said nothing. She didn't move. She just gazed across the pond at the Marshburns and Dowlings, her expression resigned and unspeakably sad. That sadness pulled at him, and it made him angrier to know that it hurt him to see her pain. He was a fool and she was a fraud. She had lied. She had betrayed his trust. She deserved to be unhappy when her actions were exposed.

"Word of your deception has disrupted the pleasure of the day. Do you wish me to take you home?"

She did not shift her gaze from the far side of the pond. "It would be best and I am sure you wish to be out of my presence as soon as possible."

"What I want to know is *why*. Why did you leave your husband? Why did you lie? Why come to Halifax?" *Why let me believe you might be drawn to me too?*

But had she? She had told him from the beginning that she had no interest in relationships or marriage. She had remained polite, returned his greetings, but not lingered to visit. It wasn't until he had used Janet as an excuse for spending time with her that she had allowed him a glimpse of her private thoughts.

She still did not return his gaze. "My reasons make no difference and are my business."

"Nonetheless, I would like to know. It might make me feel less a fool."

She did look at him then. "You have no reason to feel foolish. You are an honorable man and there was no reason for you or anyone else to doubt my story. It was simple and believable. War widows are not uncommon and often must fend for themselves when their husbands die."

"But they don't often travel across an ocean when they do."

"My husband had friends and connections beyond London. I did not wish to be discovered."

"Yet you have been."

"Yes."

Her attention still followed the Marshburns and Dowlings who now conversed with several couples who looked across the pond at her before forming tight groups to share the latest gossip. Amelia had gathered Sophie's students around her and they, too, shot inquiring glances toward their headmistress. They had stopped skating and now huddled together when Amelia returned to speak with her parents. "I believe the girls have finished skating for the day. Perhaps we should return to town."

The ride back to the Academy was far quieter than the trip out. Even the ever blunt and upfront Janet was silent. Sophie did not know what Alec had told her students when he'd informed them they were leaving, but they did not question her about Amelia's obvious revelations. She was not inclined to speak of it either, though she knew she would have to address the issue sooner rather than later.

Her thoughts raced now that the initial shock had worn off. Her secret was out. The widow, Mrs. Bennett, was really Lady Dalton, a scandalous woman who had abandoned her marriage and driven her husband to suicide. Many would agree with Lady Marshburn that she was not fit to teach their daughters how to behave in society. With a kind of numb, fatalistic clarity she accepted that it followed that many of her students would be withdrawn from her offending influence.

Yet she did not regret choosing safety over her vows. She had tried to protect her students from her own folly by pointing out that not all gentlemen were trustworthy and they needed to look beyond public flattery and charming manners. Now, she could explain why. But would they believe the brutal truth? She had told one false story already. Why would anyone believe the truth now?

Could she reveal the truth? She shuddered to think of exposing how easily she had accepted Dalton's word that it was she who drove him to uncontrollable anger. That it was her ineptitude that made him isolate her from hosting entertainments. That it was her carelessness that caused her to lose the babes she so desired.

One did not speak of such things to an unmarried innocent. But it had been that very innocence, that unquestioning devotion, that had made her accept his taunts and physical disciplines as her fault. She knew better now. She had not deserved the pain she'd suffered. Neither, she realized, did she deserve condemnation for Dalton's actions. Not even for his death. That had been his choice, not hers.

When they arrived at the Academy and Alec assisted her from the wagon, she made up her mind. She would not remain the victim of a man who had no honor. Dread soured her stomach and tightened her chest but she would tell the truth about her marriage. If people still held her in contempt, she would at least know she no longer deceived anyone.

When her students were out of the wagon she told them, "I wish to have a private word with Mr. Graham in the drawing room while you ladies put away your things and change your clothes. I will meet you in the upstairs classroom in an hour to answer any questions you have about Miss Dowling's revelations."

Mrs. Delaney came out of the kitchen when she heard everyone arrive, but Sophie assured her they would not need her or Nettie to attend them. The girls filed up the stairs and Sophie led Alec into the drawing room. She gestured for him to take the seat opposite hers before sitting and folding her hands in her lap. So many images crowded her mind.

Where to begin?

"The first time Dalton struck me was when I objected to his losing my mare in a card game."

At her words, Alec's posture stiffened and his hands clenched the arms of the chair but he did not interrupt.

Sophie held her voice steady, determined to tell the facts and not relive them as she had so often in her nightmares. "The force of it sent me to the floor. He seemed as surprised as I at his actions and begged my forgiveness, swearing it would never happen again. I believed him."

She picked at a cuticle. "It did happen again. Each time it happened, he claimed to be devastated and apologetic, always promising he would do better if only I were a better helpmate. He could be charming when not in a rage, so I kept telling myself he would reform and sought to find ways to placate him. But the frequency of his ridicule and chastisements increased until nothing I did was right. Everything I did was wrong." Sophie looked down at the untidy cuticle, then admitted her greatest sorrow. "I could not even carry a child to term."

She took a fortifying breath and met Alec's eyes. He shifted in his chair and opened his mouth to speak, but Sophie held up her hand to stop him. "Six months after our wedding, I had a dizzy spell and fell down the stairs which caused me to lose our first child. Dalton was all that was solicitous and insisted I drink a medicinal tea each morning to regain my strength. It did not help. In fact, I felt weaker. But he was adamant."

"Then, a few months later, I realized I was again with child. I was overjoyed. Dalton was furious. He told me the tea was supposed to prevent conception. I was horrified and angry that he had deceived me. We argued. He struck me again... And again." She made herself take another slow breath. "His apology afterward was so sincere that I told myself that he had wanted to spare my health by giving me more time to recover. The damage was done, though, and I lost that child, too."

Sophie clasped her hands tighter. Her throat ached but she swallowed and continued. "He then told me he did not like children, and since his title had come to him from a convoluted line that had taken the lawyers almost a year to trace, he had no desire to preserve it for future generations. He declared that he had not married to share me with demanding infants and that once I accepted that, all would be well. I was heartbroken to realize I would not be a mother, but I foolishly believed his claims that his angry outbursts were my fault. I hoped that he would change his mind about children in time. That if I tried harder, was more sympathetic, or less flawed, he would not lose control. I did try, but I did not succeed."

She raised her chin and steadied her voice. "Two years ago, a young woman approached me at a musical evening. Miss Longborough recognized Dalton as a neighbor from her childhood and was concerned for my health and safety.

She recognized the pattern of my bouts of disorientation and illness." She met Alec's gaze. "I was frightened. I was expecting again, though I'd not yet had the courage to tell Dalton."

"That fact alone convinced me that my husband would not change his ways. Dalton soon realized I was with child and he was livid. He ranted that the apothecary had lied, that I had defied him by not drinking the tea-- though I had not, for I now feared he might take his anger out on a child." She grieved for the babes whose innocent souls had been denied existence. She mourned her lack of motherhood but took solace that they would not endure a brutal father. For Dalton would have been as cruel to those babes as he had been to her.

She checked the clock on the mantle. Had it taken only fifteen minutes to expose her humiliation and failure as a wife? "In the weeks that followed that beating and miscarriage Miss Longborough convinced the Duke of Wolverton of my peril and he arranged for me to escape. Had I remained in England I could not trust that I would not be recognized by one of his friends and be forced to return to his control. I am-- was, after all, his wife. His property. The duke provided letters of introduction with a false name and passage on a ship for Halifax."

She let her head dip back against the chair and sighed. "Yet now, a whole ocean away, I have been found out, though it seems I will not be forced to return."

Chapter 12

Alec clenched his hands against the arms of the chair while Sophie chronicled the abuse she had suffered. Disgust for her husband replaced his shock and disillusion that she had abandoned her marriage.

He'd known men who did not govern their anger. He'd fought several of them. The fools took offence at the smallest imagined slight and blamed everyone else for their lack of control. Dalton should have protected his wife, not bullied her. She should not have been made to flee for her life. And now? It struck him that her husband's death meant she need not remain in hiding. That she need not remain in Halifax.

"Now that your husband is no longer a threat, will you return to England?" Alec dreaded her answer. "Are there people there you miss?"

She sat quietly, as though gathering her thoughts. It disturbed him that she had spoken without tears, without anger, without...*feeling*. She should be angry. She should be elated that she was no longer shackled to the reprobate. *Something*. Anything. Clearly, she'd learned to control her own emotions so as not to fan her husband's, and that bothered him as much as the story of her mistreatment. Alec's knuckles showed white where he clenched the wooden arms of his chair. Her dead husband deserved every minute of the time he would spend in hell.

Sophie was a strong woman of pride and determination. Would she leave? What would that mean for her? *What will it mean for me?*

Alec's belly churned and his throat ached at the thought. She belonged here. She belonged to the new life she had forged. She belonged with him.

But she doesn't.

He swallowed a great lump of bile. No matter that their recent tea idylls filled a void he'd not known he had, he had no claim on her. But he wanted one, and had since he'd watched her play a game of tug-of-war with a mongrel puppy who strayed into her back garden shortly after she moved in. Her laughter had been full of joy and delight and so contrary to the serious woman he'd met that he suspected her laughter was what had fueled his fascination with her. She so rarely laughed. He had wanted to see the playful, laughing Sophie. The one he believed was hidden behind the protective wall of caution she used as a shield.

He didn't want her to leave. He needed her here. *Sophie*. Not the careful headmistress of Mrs. Bennett's Academy for Young Ladies or the scandalous Lady Dalton of Mayfair, England. *Sophie*.

Sophie raised her head and straightened her posture. A grimace tightened her features but her eyes remained dry. "I have no family in England, so I have no reason to return. I shall not be driven from my home a second time. I shall deal with gossip and rumor however it changes my future."

Alec crossed to her chair, took her hands in his and drew her up to stand. "All will be well, Sophie. I understand why you left such a man. Others will as well."

"Most will not."

He slid his arms around her and pressed her against his chest. It was a sign of how much turmoil boiled beneath that ever-stalwart control that she allowed his comfort. When her arms slipped around his waist and she pressed her face against his heart he wanted to keep her there for all eternity.

"But the ones who count, will."

That made her chuckle, then give a choked sob before she wept against his chest.

His arms encircled her. "All will be well, Sophie. I won't desert you."

She shook her head and gave a shuddering sigh. "But you must. Now that the captain has sailed, Janet must live with you so her reputation is not tainted by my influence."

"I do not fear your influence on her. I applaud it. You are a good woman, Sophie. Do not worry about the future. You are not alone. I am here for you."

She pulled back and met his gaze, her lashes spiked with tears. She looked so woebegone he could not resist and rested his lips on hers.

He meant his kiss as a reassurance, a pledge, but then her lips softened, his clung, and warm assurance ignited into the promise of far more. His heart pounded and his breath shortened when Sophie met his kiss with fervor and a moan of desire that sent his whole being on alert. She pressed closer and her tongue met his in a duel of passionate desire. Heart pounding, breath keeping time with its frantic rhythm, Alec plundered her mouth, claiming all the long restrained need she offered until her unrestrained surrender prodded his conscience and made Alec break away.

Not now. Not here. Not when she is upset and vulnerable.

He opened his eyes and saw the dazed shock that dilated her eyes. She blinked. He straightened up and took a step back. "Sophie, I am sorry. I did not mean..."

"I know." Her breaths were as short and rapid as his. After a moment she stepped back and took a long slow breath. "Thank you."

Alec stroked Sophie's cheek. "Do not thank me for trying to comfort you, and do not be sorry for kissing me back. I have wanted to kiss you since the day we were introduced." Her eyes widened and her breath caught. "The next time we kiss you will not be so vulnerable." He smiled, then whispered, "And unless I am greatly mistaken, there will be a next time."

Her cheeks flushed but she met his gaze, then reached out to smooth his hair from his brow. "I need to go speak with my students now."

Alec watched her climb the stairs and vowed to shelter her in the storm of gossip that was sure to be unleashed across the upper citizens of Halifax.

Four questioning faces turned to her when Sophie entered the upstairs classroom. The afternoon light filtered through the window, casting long shadows on the far wall. The girls had decorated the room with vases of holly the day before, and the bright red berries had given the space a cheerful note that contrasted against the somber expressions her students wore.

"We don't believe her, Mrs. Bennett," Janet said when she stepped through the doorway. The other girls nodded their agreement. "We know your husband did not kill himself. He died fighting against the French. The English lord has mistaken you for someone else."

Sophie's throat tightened and her eyes stung in gratitude for Janet's defense, erroneous as it was. "Thank you for your loyal support, ladies, but it is true that I am Lady Dalton, not Mrs. Bennett. I am sorry to have deceived you and your families, but I hope you will understand when I explain the circumstances." Her statement had caused Janet's face to blanch until the fine sprinkle of freckles contrasted with her pale features. The other girls' faces had also drained of color before flushing into varying degrees of bright pink.

"Then you really did desert your husband?" Miss Wilkes's voice held a note of horror.

"I fled my husband, I did not desert him." Sophie took a seat at her desk and folded her hands to keep them from trembling. "Had he been in need of help or support in some way when I left him it might be considered desertion. He was not. I, on the other hand, was in danger from his mistreatment and fled for my life."

She made eye contact with each of them. "You are aware I have often spoken of how important it is for a young woman to look beyond flattery and charming smiles while courting." All four nodded, their attention unwavering. "That is because I was flattered by a charming devil who dropped his pleasing manners after we married. When I learned that his charm had been no more than a ruse, I reminded myself that the marriage vows included *for better or worse* and resolved to do my best in a bad situation. I will not shock you with the details of that situation, but suffice it to say his mistreatment was both physical and emotional." Four pair of eyes watched her, their expressions fascinated, curious, and horrified as she continued. "An acquaintance made me realize my only recourse from harm was to escape." She swallowed to moisten her dry throat. "So I did." Silence stretched for several seconds when Sophie ended her explanation.

Then, Betsy Endicott spoke quietly but with conviction. "I witnessed the mistreatment of many women around the military camps before Papa brought us to live in town. If your husband mistreated you in such a manner, you were right to leave, and I will tell Amelia Dowling so."

"Why didn't your family do something?" Georgianna Wilkes declared. "I have six brothers who will make sure whoever I marry treats me right."

"I had no family and my guardians were as misled by Lord Dalton's charm as I was. I knew no one would believe the truth. His behavior in public was entertaining and pleasant. It was only in private that he let go his control and allowed his anger free range. If Miss Longborough had not known of his true nature I don't know if I would have had the courage to leave."

Janet nodded her head. "Betsy is right. Papa and Uncle Alec always told me a man's duty is to protect his wife and family."

Caroline Hawthorne agreed. "My papa says any man who does not care for his women folk deserves to be thrashed within an inch of his life, then thrown to the pigs."

Another half hour passed before Sophie was satisfied that her students understood her choices and that many people would no longer consider her respectable. She had assured them she would understand if their parents chose to remove them from her influence. Though the girls protested, she knew better than to hope the school would not be put in peril of closure.

LADY DALTON'S DECEPTION

When she finally closed the door to her bedchamber, she sank onto the bed. She'd managed a brave front, determined not to show how very shaken she was to know that she would have to remake herself again. At least she thought she had succeeded so far as the girls were concerned. But Alec's gentle hug told her he'd seen through her attempt.

If only he hadn't kissed her.

He had offered the kiss as one gives reassurance to a frightened child but then... *Then she had leaned in*, and the kiss had deepened until her shattered past melted into yearning. Worse, it had blossomed into need. When he broke the kiss, he had been embarrassed as had she. She closed her eyes and shuddered. No matter that he claimed to have dreamt of kissing her, she feared it was pity and not desire that had fueled his reaction to her kiss. Pity and vulnerability did not lend themselves to lasting comfort.

But he also said they would share more kisses after the shock of the day faded. Would they? His gentle stroke against her cheek and the intensity of his expression nearly made her believe it. A flutter of anticipation warmed her. She wanted to believe it. Did she dare?

She wasn't ready for this. Her spirits were bruised and her heart ached. It was if she'd endured another beating at Dalton's hand. In a way she had, since his death knocked the foundation of her carefully erected life into dust. Who was she now? *A wife pretending to be a widow who was a widow who believed she was a wife*. She needed time to sort it all out.

She had been an obedient child, a compliant ward, a submissive wife. Her one act of rebellion to leave her marriage had been at the instigation and assistance of a near stranger. Even the decision to open the academy had been Margery's idea. To her dismay, Sophie could not think of any time in her life when she had acted entirely on her own. Could she be as decisive as she claimed to be? Was she as strong as she needed to be? She had to prepare for whatever came next but all she had were questions, not solutions. Her mind muddled and she couldn't think anymore. With a sigh, she curled into a ball on the counterpane. The exhaustion overwhelmed her bruised emotions and she drifted into oblivion.

When she woke the room was in darkness, but she heard voices and the sound of people moving about. The events of the morning and afternoon surfaced with consciousness and she wished she didn't have to deal with the upheaval of her carefully controlled refuge. Unfortunately, life with Dalton had taught her that wishing things were different did not make them so. She rose, lit the lamp beside her bed, then freshened her face and hair. She would have to manage. *By herself.* Her stomach lurched and ice edged prickles chilled her spine. *Could she?*

Alec had assured her she was strong, but she had learned to hide her feelings. He told her she was capable but how could he admire a woman who dithered over every decision she was forced to make? He thought her admirable, but what had she ever done to earn his respect? Until she took a stand in her own defense, she did not deserve his assurances.

If only he hadn't kissed her.

Chapter 13

The increase of whispers when Sophie and her students took their usual pew in church the next day made clear that word of the Marshburns' revelations had spread across polite society. Most people pretended not to see her nods of greeting. No one other than Alec, who took a seat on the aisle beside Janet, chose to share the pew with them. The whispers that followed in her wake stirred the air with curiosity and condemnation. *Did you hear...?*

Critical whispers about her were not new, though it had been two years since Sophie had endured them. As Lord Dalton's wife, she had not been spurned, but she had been the frequent subject of dismayed matron gossip. Dalton's public show of indulgence and affection meant that society pitied him though they praised his patience with her failings.

As she had done then, she retreated into a protective shell of assumed serenity. She refused to acknowledge her mortification when the topic of the sermon was on the sanctity of marriage. As the vicar recited passages that emphasized the duties of wives to their husbands, her embarrassment altered to irritation, then to anger. She had done all she could to be a good and proper wife. Why assume she had not? Dalton had been the one who had ignored his duties and vows. When she left her husband, she swore she would not be mistreated again. She now swore she would not accept blame for surviving Dalton's cruelty nor would she allow it to ruin the new life she had made in Halifax.

When the service ended, Sophie waited until most of the worshipers left before making her way to where the vicar met his flock at the door of the church. Her students had preceded her and she noted Betsy Endicott speaking earnestly with Amelia Dowling. Janet had cornered Eleanor and her mother.

She stepped out from the vestibule, stopped in front of the Vicar and smiled. "A most interesting sermon this morning, sir." He blinked and looked surprised that she had not tried to slip past him out of shame. "Though scripture instructs us that a husband is the head of the household and wives are to submit to his control, it also says that husbands are not to mistreat their wives and that they are to care for them as they care for themselves. I fear no one ever explained that admonition to Lord Dalton." She drilled him with her gaze. "The Bible may not encourage a woman to leave her husband but it does address the possibility. We are directed that if a wife leaves her husband she may not remarry until he dies." She paused a moment before stating, "I have not formed adulterous relationships and have not remarried." She raised her finger as she made her final point. "Please note, however, that according to Lord Marshburn, my husband is dead, so such admonitions no longer apply." She dipped her head, then turned away and descended the stairs. "I will pray that next week's sermon reflects the love and forgiveness of the holiday season."

LADY DALTON'S DECEPTION

Alec circulated among the dispersing crowd outside the church while he waited for Sophie to exit the sanctuary. He surveyed the clusters of chatting friends and wondered if he would be the only one to offer her the courtesy of continued friendship. She had barely acknowledged him when he'd taken a seat beside Janet for the service. Did she fear the congregation would assume they were more than friends if he spoke with her after the vicar's less than subtle sermon? After the kiss they'd shared he couldn't help but admit he would like to be. But would she feel the same way once she was no longer in shock and vulnerable?

Sophie had addled his brain and good sense. He'd meant to comfort her, not trespass on her need to be sheltered in a hug. When he slid his arms around her, tremors revealed how distressed the morning events had left her. He'd pressed his lips to hers in consolation but she had made that tiny whimper and pressed back. Then she'd clung to him like a lifeline and, *Dear God and all the saints combined*, he hadn't been able to resist deepening the kiss.

She had been as shaken as he by the blaze of passion that had left them both breathless. Their response had been mutual, ardent, and far too enticing to ignore. It was also untimely under the circumstances.

He frowned when he overheard Mrs. Dowling declare her satisfaction with the sermon. The Marshburns stood beside her along with two other couples. She tipped her head in the direction of the church where Sophie could be seen speaking to the vicar. "Though I wonder if it made an impression on the one person who most needed to hear it. She certainly shows no remorse that I can see." She smirked while she smoothed her gloves. "She will soon understand the error of her ways when neither Amelia nor any of her other students return to her classroom. Once the families of the boarding students receive my letters they are sure to make other arrangements for their daughters as well."

"I beg your pardon, Mrs. Dowling," Alec tipped his hat as he interrupted their conversation. "But have you questioned why a lady would change her name then travel across the sea to leave her husband? It seems apparent to me that a woman would not take such extreme measures were there not extenuating circumstances. After all, it is not unheard of for contentious spouses to agree to live apart, so why would she choose to come where she had no friends or family to take her in or support her?"

Marshburn raised an eyebrow. "Do you seek to defend her actions? I can only assume you have been taken in by her appearance as Dalton was. Lovely as she is to look at, her awkward misadventures soon made Dalton the recipient of amused pity. Our amusement faded to dismay when she did not support her husband in society by encouraging friendships or cultivating advantageous connections as she should."

Lady Marshburn added her agreement. "Mama said it was a shame Lord Dalton had married such a self-centered woman."

"Odd," Alec responded. "Though her manner is reserved, she interacts with several charities. Something I would not associate with selfishness."

Marshburn shook his head though his eyes did not waiver. "Dalton excused her inhospitality on chronic ill health, though everyone knew her illnesses were conveniently timed. He denied it of course, but her absences told a different story. Dalton was a gentleman of high spirits who was delighted when he won the hand of the season's brightest diamond only to discover her to be nothing more than a millstone around his neck. He tried to disguise his disappointment, but his friends knew the truth. He was a capital fellow who loved a woman unworthy of him though he indulged her defects with the patience of a saint."

Lady Marshburn blushed and added, "Mama told me that as soon as Lady Dalton was free of her guardian's good taste, her evening wear was more fit for the demi-monde than a lady of quality. Mama often wondered why Dalton allowed her such freedom of dress."

Lady Marshburn's description of Sophie did not fit with the quiet and modest woman he knew. He nodded in Sophie's direction. "I see nothing to question in the lady's manner of dress, nor have I seen her wear any immodest garments since her arrival. The woman you describe is not anything like the woman I have known for two years."

Marhburn's voice took on a note of sneering contempt. "I recall you were with her at the pond. You have come to know her well, have you?"

Alec scowled. "I do not appreciate your tone, sir. As her near neighbor I have observed her from a distance, and my niece is one of her boarding students for whom I acted as chaperone. The lady has lived above reproach despite her apparent need to escape her husband."

"I beg your pardon. I fear my friend's demise has left me suspicious of anyone with whom she associates." Marshburn held his ground but amended his expression. "Dalton was enthralled with his wife though she was not the woman he deserved." He met Alec's gaze and advised, "You would be wise to remove your niece from her influence as soon as possible." He touched the brim of his hat before they walked to where a coachman waited with their carriage.

Marshburn and the Dowlings had not answered the question he had raised and were unlikely to change their minds, but he believed what Sophie had told him. He'd seen the sorrow in her eyes when she spoke of the babes she had lost and remembered pain when she spoke of Dalton's recurring mistreatment.

Alec turned back to see Sophie cross the grass to where her students had gravitated together. He watched her stride past the gauntlet of disapproving faces. Marshburn was wrong. It was Sophie who had been tied to someone she hadn't deserved.

Monday dawned, chilled by northern winds but free of rain or snow. Sunlight made the remaining ground snow sparkle before melting into the underlying mud. Sophie stood at the window, disappointed but not surprised when none of her day students attended class. How long would it be before gossip letters reached the parents of her boarding students? Alec had assured her he would not remove Janet from her care, but she couldn't run the school with just one student. She watched people going about their business and reconciled herself to the inevitable upheaval in her life. There was no point in denying it. If the remaining girls were pulled from her school the only logical alternative was to change her school into a boarding house.

The influx of naval presence had caused rents in town to rise dramatically and Nettie's circumstances had been limited to the Poor Asylum. The choices were not much better for women who worked as seamstresses, milliners, or other such trades. Safe housing for women of limited means could offer Sophie a way of making a decent living.

She turned back to study the classroom where the girls practiced their penmanship. If she divided the space into two more lodging quarters the added monies meant she would be able to set aside funds for emergencies. She bit her lip at the irony. Her life in the last few days had become an emergency.

Now that she had reconciled herself to her options, she must apprise her barely hired staff of the probable changes. Oddly, the resolution disturbed her less than she would have thought. She would miss her students, but for the first time since her disastrous marriage, she did not doubt her decision.

"When you have copied this morning's poem," she told the girls, "you are to compose your weekly letter to your families. Do not think to spare them the revelations brought to light by Lord Marshburn. They should know who teaches their daughters and decide for themselves if they are willing to leave you in my care."

Janet looked up. "Uncle Alec told me I could stay."

Sophie nodded. "He informed me, as well, Miss Graham. But the other girls' families might decide otherwise. Since you do not need to write to your uncle, you are to write your thoughts in your journal." She crossed to the door. "I need to speak with the staff. Then, when I return, we shall commence your drawing lessons."

When she had explained the possible changes in the household, Nettie raised the question Sophie had tried to avoid thinking about.

"And what are we to call you, Ma'am? When people ask for your name, which do we use?"

"It will seem strange after two years, but I suppose I shall have to answer to Lady Dalton since I was never really Mrs. Bennett." Perhaps she should compromise and use Dalton's family name, Franklin. Neither idea appealed.

A spark of rebellion made her clench her hands. She was no longer married to Dalton, so why should she be obliged to retain his name? That thought sent a quiver of giddy defiance down her spine. Why could she not continue to be Mrs. Bennett?

The idea shocked her even as it took root. Her assumed name had caused no one harm nor had she taken it for any reason other than to protect herself. *Why not?* She lifted her chin and declared, "Nevertheless, I shall continue as Mrs. Bennett. Those who object will likely cut my acquaintance regardless of the name I use."

Choice made, a peculiar sense of freedom lifted her spirits as she returned to her students and their lessons.

Chapter 14

Janet arrived at Alec's doorstep Wednesday morning. She scowled just as she had when she had complained about Sophie weeks before. "The Wilkes's have removed Georgina from the academy. They are friends with the Dowlings, so they wouldn't listen to Georgina when she told them she didn't want to go."

Janet's eyes reddened and glistened with unshed tears. "Caroline wrote to her parents and told them she hopes they will let her stay. Betsy says we won't hear from her parents for at least another week, but she hopes they don't send for her either. She told them she doesn't like living in military camps and prefers living in town."

Alec held his arms out and Janet hurled herself into them before bursting into sobs. "It's not fair. Everyone is turning against her." Her tears overflowed and her voice quivered. "It's not her fault her husband was mean! If he hit me everyone would stop him, but they wouldn't help Sophie because she was married to him."

Alec agreed. "It isn't fair and it isn't right." It was a point he had made to any who criticized Sophie in his hearing He loosened his hold and stepped back to look Janet in the eye. "We will stand by her. We will remind people of what a kind woman and neighbor she has been. She will overcome this."

"I told Eleanor all about Lord Dalton and how Sophie told us to look beyond handsome faces and flattery when courting." She wiped her eyes. "We think she wanted to protect us from men like him."

"I am sure of it." Alec gave her another quick hug, then walked across the room to poke at the coals in the stove. "I think you could use a cup of tea to cheer you up, lass."

Janet wiped her eyes and nodded. Crossing the room, she took down the tea crock and scooped a portion of tea leaves into the teapot. After she set it on the table, she picked up the calico cat who wound about her legs and sat in the rocker chair. "Annabelle is getting fat."

"Annabelle is going to have kittens." Alec set two cups onto the table. "I suspect the great grey mouser they keep at the newspaper office has been to visit."

She stroked the cat in her lap, then let her hand rest on Annabelle's rounded belly. "Georgina and I think that if Sophie got married again and didn't have to be called Lady Dalton or Mrs. Bennett, people would forget about what the Marshburns said and like her again." She avoided looking at Alec. "She wouldn't have to run the academy anymore so it wouldn't matter if her students were withdrawn."

"I suspect it would matter to her, Janet. She once told me she had no intention of ever marrying again."

"That was when she thought she was still married, Uncle."

Alec froze. *Had that been her only reason?* Cold reasoning tempered his hopes and he shook his head. "When she thought she was still married, she was faithful to her promise to forsake all others despite leaving her husband's control, but I don't believe his death will change her mind. I think her husband made her wary of marriage. She has already said she will not return to England even though she would now be safe from his abuse."

"Betsy thinks you would like to court Sophie. I told her that you spend time with her because of me." She glanced up at him and a hint of a smile lit her expression. "But I do think she might be right."

Alec frowned when heat rose from his neck to his hairline and burned his ears. "Sophie doesn't want to marry again. Do not make assumptions about either of us." He stood and wrapped a towel around the handle of the kettle of boiling water to avoid his niece's slyly implied question. "I will do nothing to raise further speculation about her."

She watched him fill the teapot. "I may not know much about such matters, but I have eyes. You would court her if she allowed it. Now that she knows she is really a widow, maybe she will." She grinned up at him. "I wouldn't mind having her as my aunt."

Alec scowled. Her grin told him she had noticed the heat that burned its way to his hairline. "Just a short time ago you complained that you didn't like her."

"But you do."

"Drink your tea. I have work to do."

An hour later, Alec stared out the window of his warehouse while he waited for his manager to arrive. Clyde lay in his lap, eyes closed, purring with the loud rumble that marked his contentment. The day was overcast again, but it didn't look like snow or rain. Few people strolled along the street below this morning, though it would fill again as soon as the next ship arrived. His warehouse was situated at the invisible borderline between refined merchants and the inevitable taverns and brothels that found profit in the transient life of the military and merchant seamen. His mind was not on the view, however, but on Janet's disturbing observations earlier. Had Sophie remained distant solely because of her belief that she was still married? She had returned his kiss with a response that had left them both breathing hard.

He'd told himself that his infatuation with Sophie was no more than the natural response to a beautiful female. He had convinced himself that he had backed away when she did not encourage his interest. He had fooled himself into thinking friendship was enough.

He snorted and Clyde opened his eyes before settling back down and renewing the purring rumble. *Admit it, fool.*

He had spent too much time looking down from his back window in hopes of seeing her tend the garden or entertaining her students' families with an alfresco afternoon. He had watched for small opportunities to greet her. He had used Janet as an excuse to spend time with her in private. Or as private as one could be in a drawing room with staff and students moving about their business.

The Marshburn revelation had left Sophie badly shaken, and the withdrawal of so many students further battered her spirits. How long would it be before she recovered from her shock? How long before a shared kiss did not make him feel guilty of taking unfair advantage? Waiting for the woman to recover might well drive him into madness. *Blast and damnation.*

He had lied to himself. He leaned forward and pressed his head against the cold windowpane. If he had observed any other man watching her that way he would have driven him off for trespassing on her privacy.

She kissed me back.

It always came back to that. Patience stretched only so far after a woman kissed a man back.

"Janet is right, Clyde. I do want to court Sophie. More than that, I want to marry her. But how do I convince her that marriage doesn't have to be a prison of pain and disappointment? How do I make her believe marriage to me offers security and protection?"

He scratched the back of the cat's ears and huffed a sigh of frustration. Doubtless his employees would snigger in amusement if they knew he shared his private thoughts with the great orange tom cat.

"Problem is, I can't forget that kiss."

Their response had been mutual, ardent, and far too enticing to ignore. It was also untimely under the circumstances. He ran his fingers through his hair in frustration.

I shouldn't have kissed her.

Sophie folded the letter she held. Oddly, she was relieved that there was no longer any question of whether she would have students in the future. Caroline's parents had come for her two days prior with the intention of sending her to England under the supervision of a well-placed cousin. The Endicotts' letter apprised her that Betsy was to take up residence with the Jaspers until her parents returned in a month's time. That left only Janet. Sophie had no other option but to close the school and take in general boarders.

Janet would not be happy. Neither would Alec. *But needs be as needs must.*

Janet should go to live with her uncle by the end of the week. And once Janet was gone Sophie would have no reason to see either of them other than chance meetings along the street. That thought made her lips tremble and her eyes sting. She swallowed past her aching throat and turned to a fresh page in her ledger. But instead of columns and numbers, all she saw was the warmth in Alec's eyes before he kissed her. Heat flared and spread at the memory. They had not seen each other for several days and she would have avoided him had he made an attempt to see her. *He had not.*

Was she disappointed that he had not? Now that she was truly free of her marriage, she was legally and morally free to encourage the interest of other men. Did she want to encourage Alec? The idea sent a shiver along her spine. Simply being in the same room with him left her breathless. He was handsome and attentive. His kiss ignited needs she'd thought buried forever. Did Alec's physical appeal mean she was still as foolish as she had been with Dalton?

Sophie frowned. *Enough of this.* She opened her ledger and attempted to review her expenses until Nettie entered the office and set a tea tray on the desk. "Ma'am, do you really plan to change the school into a ladies' boarding house?"

Sophie looked up. "It is necessary. Without students it is impossible to continue the school."

Nettie twisted her hands together and bit her bottom lip. "If you don't mind me asking, how much will the rent be? You see, Ma'am, when Mrs. Babcock sent me to fetch more flour this morning, the girl who assisted me said she shares a room with another girl from the shop. But it is near the docks, and with the days as short as they are, they have to be extra careful when they return in the dark." She clasped her hands. "I didn't say nothing about you changing things, but

I wondered if they would be able to share a room here if you do."

Sophie tried to unscramble her thoughts and focus on Nettie's question. "I have yet to calculate what I must charge to remain solvent."

Nettie's question reminded Sophie how frightened she and Margery had been those first nights after they arrived in Halifax. Taverns and brothels lined the streets near the docks where the sailors and privateers sailed in and out of port. By day, their accommodations were not so dangerous so long as one avoided the less savory sections, but the atmosphere around the inn had become much more menacing once darkness fell. She had not ventured beyond Mr. Wiseman's pawn shop, and they had been greatly relieved once she had purchased the academy property. If she kept her rents low might she provide those shop girls a safer place to live? She must include that in her evaluations.

"I shall prepare my figures and let you know once I have decided."

Nettie bobbed a curtsey. "Thank you, ma'am." She turned to leave, then looked back. "Mr. Graham saw me in the garden and asked me to tell you he is taking Miss Graham to the shoemaker after her music lessons tomorrow."

Her heart leapt, then plunged. *She was a fool.* Her hand trembled as she took a sip of her tea. The indisputable and disturbing truth was that Alec would still be her neighbor after he took Janet to reside with him. In all the time she had lived here, she had not allowed herself to dwell on how much she was attracted to her neighbor. *Not often, anyway.* Now it was all she could think of. She closed her eyes and clutched her teacup tightly. She could not give in to her emotions. She must make practical choices that did not depend on others. She must stand alone.

It made no sense to put off the inevitable. Despite the lateness of the hour, she left her office. The night air chilled Sophie's nose and dirt clung damply to her half-boots as she made her way across the garden to Alec's back door. She'd not been alone with him since she had reacted so desperately to the kiss he'd meant to comfort her. Despite the cold, her cheeks burned when she thought about how blatantly she'd clung to him, how wantonly she had returned and deepened his kiss. Her heart fluttered. He'd told her he would kiss her again. Would he think that was why she had come to his door tonight?

She stopped short of knocking at the thought. Should she have sent him a formal note to explain that she was closing the school and that Janet could no longer remain? She turned, ready to do just that when Alec opened the door. Her stomach flipped and her breath caught when he took a startled step back and a well-rounded calico cat slipped past his legs out into the yard.

Chapter 15

"Sophie? Is something wrong?" Alec's eyes pinned her with concern before he reached out, clasped her hand, and drew her inside.

"Nothing unexpected," she blurted. "But the Endicotts are removing Betsy from the school." She shifted her gaze away from the intensity of his. "It is clear I will have to close the school and Janet will need to come live with you."

Alec gave her wrist a gentle tug and pulled her into his embrace. "I am sorry, Sophie. Are you sure you must close the school? Given time, people will realize you did what was necessary to protect yourself and you will have students again."

Sophie pulled back. It was too tempting to allow him to hold her. It was too tempting to hope that time alone would solve her dilemma. "No, they won't. My actions go against all society holds dear. A woman accepts her life as a man's wife and is loyal to him no matter what she must endure. It is why the marriage vows include the phrase *for better or worse*. I broke my vow and if I broke that sacred vow what other vows might I break? I understand their concerns. It is why I hid my past."

She stepped away and rested her hands on the back of a nearby chair. "I own the building but have pawned the last of my jewelry to furnish it. It is my only option. I must have income to live, so I have decided to turn the school into a boarding house for women."

An arrested expression flitted across Alec's face before he moved a step closer and lifted her hand into his once more. "You have other options, you know." He pressed his lips into her palm. "You could marry me." He looked pleased with himself, then compounded her humiliation by assuring her, "You would be back in the fold of respectability and in no need of taking in boarders of any sort."

She jerked her hand from between his and held it up to stay his advance. "No."

Alec frowned. "I am not like Dalton, Sophie. I would never raise a hand to you."

"I know that." A tremor of shock raced through her to realize she did. He was kind, thoughtful, protective and caring. She trusted Alec to be the man she had come to know. But it did nothing to quell the devastation of his well-meant but mortifying offer.

Her heart ached to know he was everything she had hoped for in her youth, yet she must refuse his noble gesture because he deserved better than the flawed woman she was. She gripped the chair back again lest he tempt her into taking the coward's way around her actions. "I cannot rely on anyone but myself to deal with the consequences of my exposed behavior. You will not sacrifice yourself for my sake."

"It is no sacrifice, Sophie. I have admired you from the day we were introduced and our visits in recent months have only raised my affection and respect for you." His mouth quirked and his gaze heated. "And I like kissing you."

"You are a man. Men like to kiss." Sophie's face flamed. "You are also protective and you want to save me from the consequences of my past. But I have to deal with it on my own. You need to protect Janet, not me. Remaining with me will damage her prospects." She released her hold on the chair and turned toward the door. "Your intentions are admirable, Alec, but you can help me most by having Janet live with you." Sophie's hand trembled when she reached for the knob but she opened the it and left before he could argue further. Before he could see the tears that burned her eyes.

Alec gaped at Sophie's abrupt exit. Bloody hell, did she think he was some kind of noble saint whose *only* reason for marrying her was to protect …?

Her eyes had narrowed and shuttered when he'd blundered on with assurances that she would be respectable *again*.

I am a mindless fool.

Yes, it was an advantage to her, but it certainly wasn't why he wanted to marry her. But now she thought it was. Worse, the stubborn woman would probably try to cut all ties with him once Janet was removed from her influence.

He snagged his coat from the peg and strode out the door after her.

That can't happen.

He crossed the open space and didn't bother knocking when he reached her back door but marched through the kitchen past the startled cook. He caught up to Sophie just as she opened the door across from her office. "Sophie, wait!"

She turned, her eyes wide and red-rimmed, her stance that of a fox run to ground. "There is nothing more to say, Alec. I shall manage without your help or pity. Take Janet home and leave me alone."

"I don't pity you." He reached out to stroke her cheek, but she flinched, and her distrust sliced at his heart. His voice barely made it past the constriction of his throat. "Don't cringe from me, Sophie. I would never hurt you."

"I know that." She lifted her hand toward him, but quickly pulled back and wrapped her arms around her waist. A tear slipped down her cheek. "I didn't mean to flinch."

That small admission gave him hope. "You should know I would never offer marriage out of pity. I admire and care about you. I want to make you happy." He sent her a tentative smile. "I want to make us both happy."

Her lips quivered, but she shook her head. "No matter your intentions, your attempt to help would hurt me more than you could ever know." She blinked and another tear escaped. She took a deep breath. "I am too dependent on others. I have never done anything for myself, never objected to what others told me I should do. I didn't even flee for my life on my own initiative. If Charlotte Longborough had not insisted I protect myself I would have endured Dalton's abuse until the day I died. A day that would have come sooner if I had not followed her advice."

Alec fisted his hands to keep from reaching for her again.

Her mouth pulled into a rueful half-smile. "Life in Halifax has been so different from what I knew in England. I was proud of my school, and of how it had grown since it opened, but even that was Margery's idea. A residential boarding house may not be much different from a boarding school, but I thought of it myself." She shrugged her shoulders and finally met his gaze. "I must find my own way as I never have. If that fails, I shall take in washing if I must." Determination and apology shone from her eyes as clearly as the tone of her voice did not waver. "I will not take shamed refuge in a marriage of convenience. It wouldn't be fair to either of us."

Her words silenced his protest. What was unfair was that such a capable woman thought following the guidance of others made her weak-willed. He had been equally determined not to accept help from Rory when he left the farm to undertake life on his own. He had succeeded, and so would Sophie. She was so much stronger than she gave herself credit for.

He reached out to stroke her cheek and this time she did not pull away. "If you insist you must manage on your own to believe in yourself I will respect that, but don't expect me to walk away, either. I will still come by for tea until you can trust in yourself as well as me." He cupped her face in his hands and whispered, "My offer is not for convenience. It is genuine and permanent. You have only to say yes if you change your mind and we shall wed." He slipped his arms around her and pulled her closer. "I look forward to that day. And I look forward to more kisses until then."

Her eyes widened with alarm which made him chuckle. "You have declared you are not a merry widow, so I'll not press for more than kisses. But there is no reason we cannot enjoy kisses until you feel you have succeeded. I can be a patient man. I will be there when you succeed... and any time in between." He leaned down and kissed her deeply, then turned on his heel and strode away before his patience was tested any more.

"Tell Janet I will come for her at midday tomorrow.

Chapter 16

Three months later

Sophie led her latest boarder to the corner room at the end of the hall.

"Welcome to the Bennett Boarding House." Sophie handed Miss Ingersoll the key after opening the door to room five. Each door now displayed painted numbers on the upper center to match the brass keys hanging in the cabinet in her office. "As you can see, Mr. Pike has already delivered your trunk."

The woman towered over Sophie, her frame as solid and strong-boned as Mr. Pike's. Perhaps a decade older than Sophie, she declared herself to be an aspiring artist whose recent inheritance allowed her to break away from disapproving dictates of her unmarried brother. A wisp of honey brown hair curled beneath her bonnet's edge which had been trimmed with a ribbon the same indigo as her dress.

"Breakfast is served at seven each morning. Supper is at six in the evening. The parlor is available for visitors, though no callers are admitted later than eight, nor are they allowed upstairs. The doors are locked at ten each night."

Sophie had worried that her notoriety would prevent her from making a success of the boarding house, but the shop girls who now rented her rooms cared more about room rates than the whispers that followed Sophie when she crossed paths with former students. A letter from Margery had revealed the actual events that had led to Dalton's fatal fall from the upper floor of their house. He had not committed suicide, but the truth would not change public opinion, so she did not choose to try. She would focus on the future and not the past. She did hope that, in time, the whispers would fade and the last of the rooms would be filled.

Miss Ingersoll had taken her room at the recommendation of Mary Gordon, the seamstress who occupied room four. The two shop girls Nettie told her about now shared a room upstairs and room three housed Miss Taylor who painted chinaware for a local merchant.

Other than the alteration in the classroom, little had changed since she'd closed the school. Samplers still decorated the walls of her office but they now reflected Miss Gordon's embroidery samples. A newly hung shelf displayed several of Miss Taylor's cup designs.

Miss Ingersoll dipped her head in acknowledgement as she took the key. "Thank you. I am sure all will be satisfactory." She took a step, then turned back. "I would appreciate it if you did not answer any inquiries about my presence here. My brother does not approve of my decision to live independently and may follow in hopes of changing my mind." Her eyes met Sophie's and her voice held a determined note. "Now that I have finally broken away, I shall not return."

Sophie's throat closed in alarm. "Will he force you to go home? If that is the case, perhaps you should return before he follows you."

Miss Ingersoll frowned. "He may threaten to, but he cannot. And I do not wish to argue with him anymore. He has never tolerated my efforts at what he terms useless and silly paint daubs." Her voice quivered, then her fingers curled and she took a slow breath. "I am of age and now have adequate independent means from my widowed aunt." She raised her chin and met Sophie's gaze without blinking. "I left him a note in order to depart without a fuss. I am not nearly the fool he thinks I am." With that assurance, she crossed the threshold, and quietly closed the door.

Sophie returned to her office, her mind in a turmoil at the thought of confronting a stranger determined to bring his sister home. Should she insist Miss Ingersoll find a different place to stay? The woman seemed more resolute than worried. Perhaps it was true that she was simply tired of arguing with her brother. Sophie stacked the receipts and put her ledger into the desk drawer. Five boarders meant her ledgers now reflected the barest of profits.

I need Miss Ingersoll.

She took a deep breath. I can do this. I *have* to do this.

An hour later Janet stuck her head around the office door. "I'm here but Uncle Alec has a meeting and can't come."

Alec had convinced Sophie to continue tutoring Janet and they still shared a pot of tea the days Janet took her lessons. She had been humming this past hour in anticipation of their time together. She smiled extra brightly but stopped humming. "No matter. Begin your scales and I shall be there in a moment."

He had not mentioned marriage again, but his words were never far from her mind.

And kisses. They were never far from her mind either.

Or from his.

Janet's lessons served as an excuse for frequent visits. Somehow, the staff was busy whenever he arrived. And, somehow, he always managed to find the opportunity to cajole kisses from her before he took his leave.

Those kisses raised her passions but played on her conscience. To her guilty dismay, she allowed them. *Wanted them.* Yet, she dared not explore them further. Her pride would not allow her to become a widow of easy virtue any more than it would allow her to make a convenient marriage to erase her scandal. She refused to take advantage of Alec's protective heart. He deserved far more than someone to be rescued from her scandalous actions.

Sophie stepped into her bed chamber to wash her hands. Even if she ignored her own arguments and admitted it was what her heart craved, she hadn't the courage to broach the subject after refusing his offer months earlier. It would be too bold.

Sophie signed the letter she had just completed in answer to Margery when a gentleman of means entered and stepped across the foyer to the office. He was large, well dressed, and smiled at Sophie with all the charm of a man used to getting his way when she stopped at the doorway. "May I help you?"

"Good afternoon. I believe Miss Astrid Ingersoll is staying here. Would you inform her that her brother has arrived to escort her home?"

A vein just below his jaw flickered and pulsed, revealing annoyance behind his pleasant request. His smile reminded Sophie of Dalton in his most convincing role of gentlemanly behavior, but the determined glint behind his practiced charm made her nerves quake and her lungs seize.

Miss Ingersoll had not seemed fearful of physical harm in denying her brother, but Sophie knew from experience how that could change without warning. How was she to placate him while protecting Miss Ingersoll? What if his annoyance erupted into violence?

Miss Ingersoll had been adamant she would not return to her brother's home. Would he bodily remove her? She was a large woman, but her brother was even larger. Miss Ingersoll had requested Sophie's discretion and she needed Miss Ingersoll to stay.

She willed her features into polite inquiry, then cleared her throat as she came to her feet behind the desk. "Did you say Ingersoll? I have no boarder by that name who is leaving."

A flash of fury tightened his eyes and she recognized the bully behind the false manner. Alarm rushed up and down her spine but she held her ground. The progression of Janet's scales filtered from the parlor revealing that they were not alone.

Sophie was not surprised when he feigned a rueful chuckle to conceal his irritation and lifted his hands in a gesture of surrender. "I've no doubt she has asked you to conceal her presence. We had a silly disagreement and she flounced off in high dudgeon, but if you would just fetch her down I am sure we will reconcile and she will agree to return home."

Her throat dried but she would not betray Miss Ingersoll's trust. How could she when she understood too well the tyrant behind the charm? "As I stated before, I have no boarder by that name who intends to check out."

His charm slipped and his smile faded. "I dislike accusing a lady of falsehoods, but I do not believe you." He leaned forward and spoke softly, "I have confirmed that the post chase delivered her and her trunk to this house, so I suggest you do as I ask and bid her prepare for the journey home." His now threatening glare sent shivers along Sophie's spine until they splintered and shot to the ends of her hands and the souls of her feet.

She clutched the edge of the desk to keep from backing away from the menace behind his softly issued command. Dalton had used similar tactics and she had always given in rather than chance his retaliation. But when she had escaped his control, she had sworn she would not be mistreated again.

Never again.

Despite her pounding heart, she met his irate gaze. Mr. Ingersoll had no authority over her. His sister was well past her majority, so he had no legal authority over her either. Anger flared and fueled her determination. "I do not take orders from strange men who enter my premises demanding access to women who may or may not reside here." She locked her jaw and forced herself to breathe. "Since there is no reason for you to remain, I must ask you to leave."

He stared at her for several seconds, his mouth a grim line, and Sophie's heart stuttered and crashed about her chest as she returned his baleful glare.

"Mrs. Bennett, do you know if... Oh, I'm sorry, Ma'am." Nettie stopped in the doorway. Her eyes widened, then her startled gaze bounced between Sophie and Mr. Ingersoll before she took a step back into the hall.

With all the smooth fluidity of ingrained habit, Mr. Ingersoll's lips had widened into a disarming smile as he turned to see who had witnessed their tense standoff. When he saw that Nettie was a servant his expression shifted into indifference.

"It is quite alright, Nettie." Sophie took another determined breath. "The gentleman was just leaving."

Mr. Ingersoll shot her a look that belied his apparent cooperation. "I shall be at the George Inn. When you see my sister, be sure to pass on my message." He then settled his hat on his head and strode through the front door without looking back.

Sophie sank into her chair and closed her eyes. Shudders shook her shoulders and her stomach threatened to cast her breakfast onto the floor. Dear heavens, she'd ordered that man to leave *and he left*. She took a deep breath and let it out slowly. The trembling in her shoulders eased. Another breath, then realization hit, and her stomach settled. *I did it.* She opened her eyes. *I did it.*

Nettie stood just inside the door. "Are you alright, Mrs. Bennett? I didn't mean to interrupt."

Sophie absorbed the strange sense of satisfaction that settled with her heartbeat. A triumphant grin bloomed. "I am fine. Excellent, in fact. What was it you wanted to know?"

Chapter 17

Alec knocked at Sophie's kitchen door, then greeted the cook when she admitted him. The midday sun cast soft shadows through the high cloud cover and a brisk breeze sent a dry leaf scuttling across the yard.

"Good afternoon, Mrs. Babcock. How is the new boarder working out?"

"Miss Ingersoll is no trouble at all. She and Miss Taylor have become thick as thieves since she found out Miss Taylor paints those pretty flowers on cups. Miss Ingersoll paints watercolors."

The cook grinned as she removed her apron and hung it on the peg on the wall. "If you'll excuse me, I am off to the butcher's to fetch a shoulder of beef. Mrs. Delaney went to the mercantile for more candles and Nettie is weeding the garden."

Alec grinned back. He was fooling no one in this house. The staff made no secret about their match-making. Nor did Janet. The only one not cooperating was Sophie, though she did return his kisses with gratifying enthusiasm when the staff was occupied and she believed no one would see.

Patient as he tried to be, he wanted more than the hidden kisses she allowed him. He wanted marriage. But after she refused his offer he had promised not to pressure her on the matter. Was he a fool for hoping that once all the rooms were rented she would see her own worth, that she might change her mind? Was he demented for chancing she would?

From the parlor came the melody of Janet's latest assigned piece. He had been hard put to fit in this hour but refused to lose another chance to spend time with Sophie. After missing her lesson the week before, he had made it a point to make time for attending today. He crossed the kitchen and paused at the doorway.

Sophie sat on the bench beside Janet. "Excellent. You need only continue practicing for more fluid pacing."

"Sophie is right. Practice is the key to mastering anything."

They both turned to face him but Alec saw only Sophie and his heart hitched. Something about her had changed. She glowed with a confidence he'd not seen in her before. Her determination had always been there, but so had her doubts. Something made her eyes sparkle and her mouth quirk as though holding back a delightful secret that had nothing to do with Janet's lessons. Whatever it was, the change sent his blood racing to parts best ignored. She was glorious.

"Did you hear the entire piece or should Janet play it again?"

Alec had lost all awareness of his niece, but Sophie's question made him aware that Janet had witnessed his reaction. She sent him an amused gleam and knowing smile. He cleared his throat. "Yes, please. I just arrived."

"Again, then, Janet. You'll do fine." Sophie rose from the bench and laid a light hand on Janet's shoulder before moving to the sofa. She even moved with more confidence.

Janet wiped her hands on her skirts and placed them above the keys. Though the pace was slower than he'd heard it played by others, she finished without error.

"You are progressing well, Lass."

"Thank you, Uncle." Janet glanced between him and Sophie before she rose from the bench. Her eyes danced with a combination of pleasure and mischief he recognized all too well before she turned to Sophie. "Might I borrow Nettie to accompany me so I can return a book Elinor loaned me?"

Sophie nodded and Janet hurried away to find Nettie.

Satisfied that they were alone, Alec leaned forward. "What happened?"

Sophie's eyebrows rose. "What do you mean?"

"Something has lit a spark in you. Tell me about it."

Her eyes widened, then she flushed. "I look different?" She clasped her hands together under her chin and closed her eyes. When she opened them again a small smile lifted the corners of her mouth. "I suppose it is because I did not betray Miss Ingersoll's presence to her brother last week." She met his startled gaze and declared, "I ordered him to leave... *and he did.*"

Alec stiffened. "What did he do?" If the man had threatened Sophie he would track him down and throttle him.

"He told me he'd come to take her home, but I knew she did not want to go back, so I told him no one was leaving. I didn't lie, but I didn't admit she was here. When he didn't believe me and ordered me to get her I realized he had no right to order me about in my own home. It made me angry, so I told him to leave." Pride and delight lit her face. "I was terrified, but I didn't give in. He was a big man, even bigger than you, but I ordered him to leave." She met his gaze, eyes shining and wonder in her voice. "I did it."

Alec's tension melted away and he rested his hands on her shoulders, "Of course you did, and I am not surprised, either. You are a strong woman, Sophie Bennett, and a determined one. I take it he did not return."

"No. And Miss Ingersoll went to see him after I told her he had come looking for her. I gather they had one final argument in which she told him to hire a housekeeper and a cook if he wanted looking after since she was remaining in Halifax to enjoy her daubs and brushes. He left Halifax and she is still here."

Alec pulled her into a light embrace. He wanted to crush her to him, to tell her he would defend her against any and all who would threaten her, but this was her moment. She had done it. He was in awe of her. "Well done, Sophie." He kissed her forehead. "I always knew you were a brave woman and it took courage to stand up to him."

Sophie nestled close, drinking in the encouragement of his *well done.* The touch of his lips to her forehead warmed her heart and made her proud. She'd seen his protective response when she spoke of Mr. Ingersoll's intent. If things had not gone well he would have defended her. But he had listened to her full story. Had understood that her success in facing the man, the pride that had filled her, were all the more gratifying because she had acted on her own.

She eased back and drank in the warmth and tenderness in his eyes. Dalton's abuse had made her afraid to trust, but she trusted Alec. Even better, he had taught her to trust herself.

He didn't question her ability to make her own way. He talked to her. He made her laugh. His kisses left her breathless. He filled the empty well of her woman's soul and she resolved to not let one mistake cause her to make another. She would no longer deny herself a happy future because of her unhappy past.

She lifted her hands to frame his face and watched his eyes when she whispered, "Yes."

Question lifted his brow before his eyes darkened and he grinned when he caught her meaning. "We'll have the banns read on Sunday."

Sophie snuggled closer and she touched her lips to his. "I could not be a merry widow, but I believe I will be a very merry wife."

The tender warmth in his eyes shifted to heat and he flashed a triumphant grin. "My darling lass, you are marvelous." Then he slipped his hand to the back of her neck and settled in for a kiss to curl her toes and scandalize the staff... if they had not been conveniently out running errands.

Epilogue

December, 1818

Sophie looked up when a blast of frigid air shot across the kitchen. Alec backed into the room holding a wooden box filled with brown paper wrapped packages. A thin layer of snow dusted his hat and shoulders and the cold air had reddened his nose and cheeks.

"Not more presents! You will spoil the girls beyond repair." Sophie tried to adopt an expression of stern disapproval, but the laughter in her voice ruined the effect. How could she object when she knew how much happiness it brought him to dote on those he loved.

"Where are they?"

"Janet is making paper dolls with them in their room."

Little Charlotte was unlikely to be dressing the paper figures five-year-old Margery had begged Janet to make for her. Instead, their busy two-year-old preferred the hilarious task of stacking wooden blocks until they toppled over. Her chortling laughter floated down the stairwell.

Alec hid the box in the pantry and removed his coat and hat. Crossing to where she stood by the work table, he took Sophie into his arms and nuzzled her neck. "Then we have a few minutes alone." His lips traced their way up and around until he captured her mouth. The teasing nibbles warmed, then heated until Sophie melted into his embrace. He whispered into her ear and her entire body flushed with the promise of the night ahead.

Clattering footsteps on the stairs warned them that he'd been seen coming home. A wry expression crossed his features before Alec turned to catch the little girls who rounded the staircase and flew through the kitchen door.

"Papa!

Alec scooped them both into his arms and gave their cheeks smacking kisses. "Have you been good today? No fusses or quarrels?"

Sophie laughed. "Of course they were good. It is too near Christmas for them to misbehave."

Tears stung her eyes at the sight of the man she loved holding the babes they had made. She had thought this overflowing joy lost to her forever. She wrapped her arms around her torso where their third child would soon begin to show. This innocent soul would also grow and thrive with Alec as its doting father. Perhaps a boy this time? No matter. Alec's protective love held no limits and they were a family.

The one they were meant to be.

Also by
Leslie V. Knowles

THE WOLVERTON WORLD

Scandalizing the Duke
The Duke of Wolverton never expected his calm proper life to be disrupted by a compulsive rescuer, her dog, or a lady in peril.

Chasing Scandal
Agent of the Crown Tristan Sheffield's mission to uncover a traitor is complicated by an abducted child and the woman who believes he is the kidnapper.

Scandal's Choice
Unconventional spinster Elizabeth Longborough's marriage of convenience to disabled Major Warliegh becomes less convenient when the past he thought buried arrives at their door.

Lady Dalton's Deception
(a WolvertonWorld novella)
Lady Sophronia Dalton fled her abusive husband, changed her name and claimed to be a widow, but what if her secret identity is exposed?

Biography

I grew up in Southern California where my husband and I raised our two children before he passed away. Our daughter is a cake artist and is the mother of three grown sons. Our son is an aerospace engineer who made watching The Big Bang Theory seem oddly familiar.

When I am not writing, I enjoy reading, painting, photography... and far too many computer games of solitaire.

I am not done with the Wolverton World, so check my website at **leslievknowles.com for news about what is coming next.**

Also, I'd love it if you posted a review at your favorite book source site.

www.ingramcontent.com/pod-product-compliance
Lightning Source LLC
LaVergne TN
LVHW011711060526
838200LV00051B/2858